Mom's
1st Year of
Homeschooling
Handbook

Name: & Age:

Address:

Phone & Email:

INSTRUCTIONS

You are now a HOMESCHOOL MOM!
This is your "Mommy Workbook"
It is a Study Guide,
Personal Planner, Journal
& Coloring Book!

Your children will see your example and take their work more seriously too. You will need a stack of good books to accompany this Handbook.

Look around your house for books you would LOVE to read. Buy some new books. Go to the library. Choose a devotional, a cookbook, a parenting book, a book to help you learn new skills, a book to help you enrich your marriage, something that inspires you, a novel, a biography, and some How-To guides.

Supplies Needed:
Drawing pens, nice colored pencils, smooth markers. (Don't let the kids run off with your supplies.)

THIS WILL BE SO FUN.

You have a lot to learn about

Homeschooling!

You and your child are on a learning Journey together!
This book helps you to learn how to embrace your new role
and be an <u>example</u> to your child as you educate yourself!

Choose SIX Books To Read & Study!

1. Write down the titles on each cover below.
2. Keep your stack of books in a safe place.
3. Be ready to read a few pages from 3 or 4 of your books daily.
4. Complete a few pages each day in this Handbook.

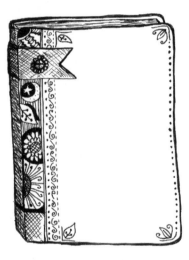 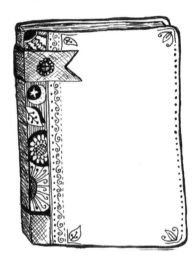 

Mom's Coloring Time

Coloring beautiful pictures and doodling
relieves stress and helps with creativity & relaxation.

CANDY

RUSSIAN SAMOVAR

CUPCAKE

TEA

COOKIES

SUGAR

JAM

TEA

JAM

"The true sign of intelligence is not knowledge but imagination." ~ Albert Einstein

A New Day!

My Verse, My Song or My Prayer...

What Matters Most...

Prayer List

Reading Time

Sit down with a few books from your stack.

Write, draw or copy the things you want to remember.

Plans & Perspective

"The home is the first and most effective place to learn the lessons of life: truth, honor, virtue, self control, the value of education, honest work, and the purpose and privilege of life." -McKay

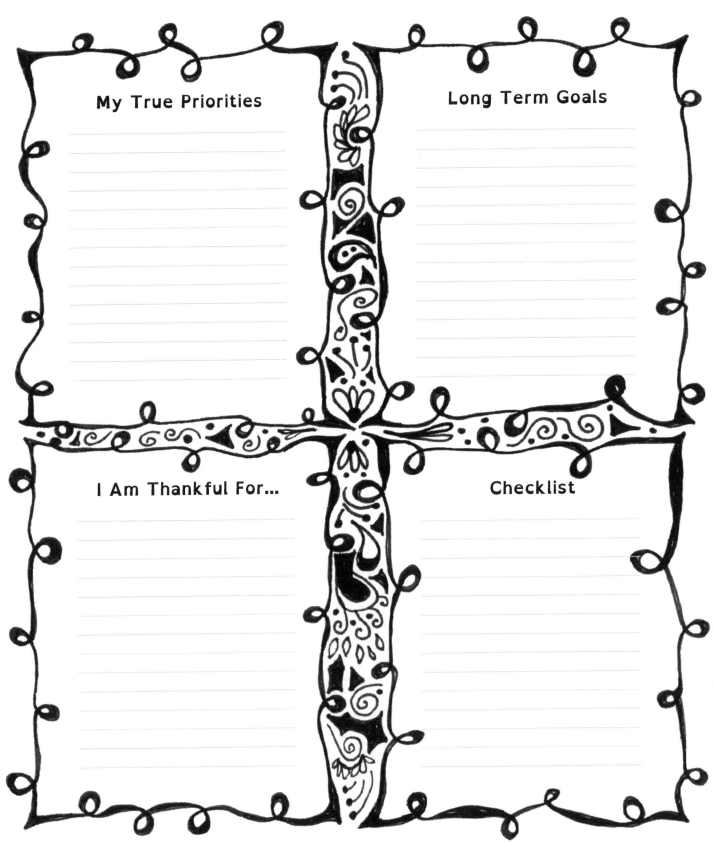

My True Priorities

Long Term Goals

I Am Thankful For...

Checklist

A Vision for Your Life

What is your vision, and what are you doing to archive it in everyday life?

_____

_____

_____

_____

Your calling and purpose is unlike any other.
Ask God for His plans for your life. Ask God for wisdom,
guidance and strength to fulfill your purpose today.

Draw a picture of your dreams for this day,
for your future, for yourself, for your home,
your marriage or for your family.

Mom's Coloring Time

Coloring beautiful pictures and doodling
relieves stress and helps with creativity & relaxation.

Mom's Illustrated TO-DO List

Menu Planning

Open up an old-fashion cookbook!

_____

_____

_____

_____

_____

_____

Shopping List

_____

_____

_____

_____

_____

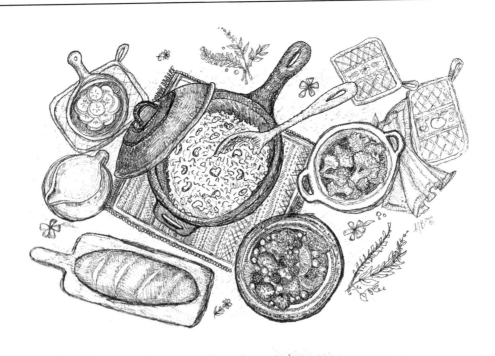

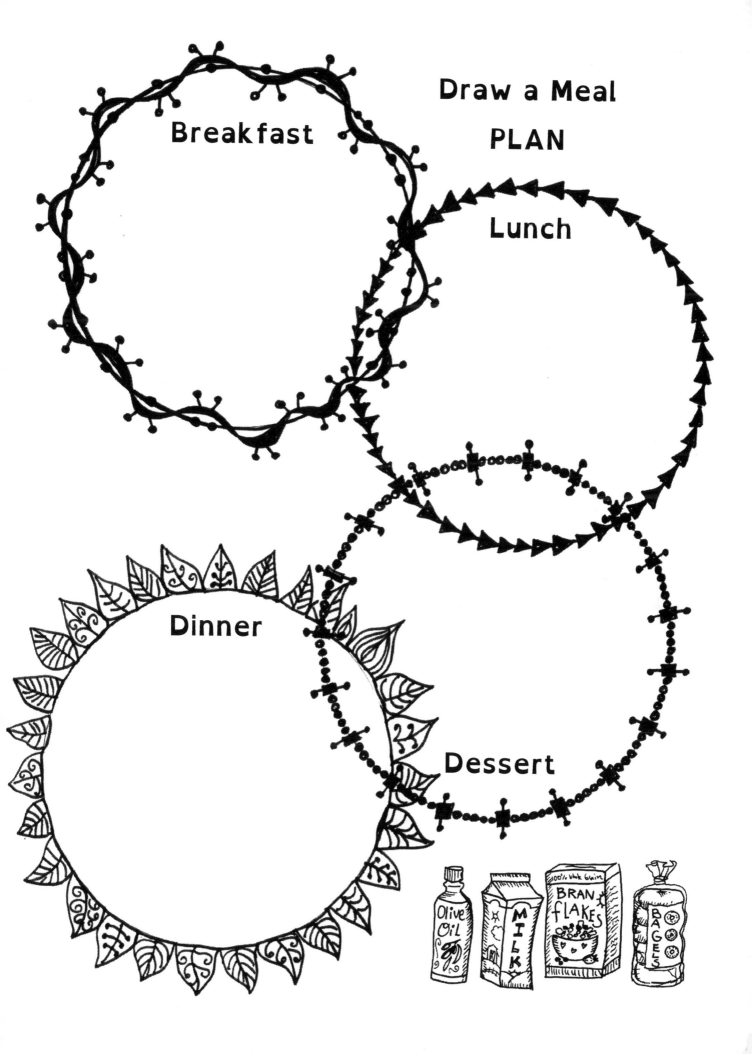

Breakfast

Draw a Meal
PLAN

Lunch

Dinner

Dessert

Recipe:

_____

Serves:

Prep Time:

Ingredients:

Instructions:

- In a bowl, combine the banana, eggs and cinnamon.
- Mix/mash until the mixture becomes all smooth. You can use a fork or a potato masher to achieve that.
- Grease your pan with a little bit of oil or butter.
- Heat your stove to a low to medium setting.
- Pour ¼ of the batter in your pan and cook for about 1½ minutes on both sides.
- Serve as is or garnish with anything you like banana slices with cinnamon and honey.

Shopping List:

"Recipe for genius: More of family and less of school, more of parents and less of peers, more creative freedom and less formal lessons." ~Raymond Moore

Mommy Math Time

Math is something that Kids need help with.

Go get a kid and show them how to do some math here:

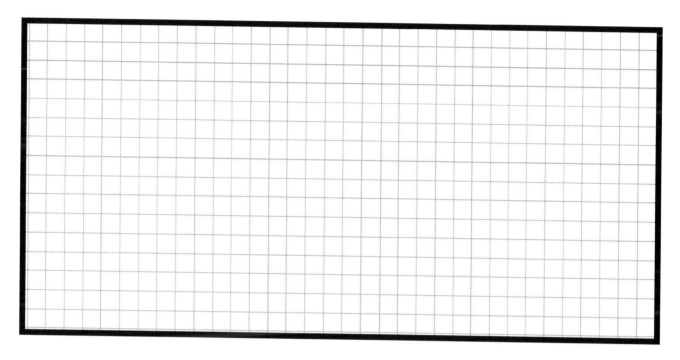

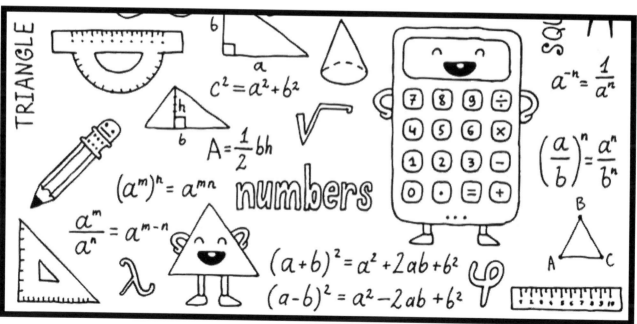

"Everything I am interested in, from cooking to electronics, is related to math. In real life you don't have to worry about integrating math into other subjects. In real life, math already is integrated into everything else." ~ Hoffstrom

Ideas for Fun & Learning Together

Reading Time

Sit down with a few books from your stack.

Write, draw or copy the things you want to remember.

Mom's Coloring Time

Coloring beautiful pictures and doodling
relieves stress and helps with creativity & relaxation.

Listening Time

Listen to an audio book or classical music or
ask someone to read a story to you while
you color and draw on the next page.

What are you listening to?

_____

TITLE:

STARS:

Screen Time!
Watch a Documentary, Educational Program, Movie, or Tutorial.

My Review of this Film:

Draw a Scene from the video:

Rating:
AWFUL
BAD
LAME
YUCKY
OKAY
NICE
GOOD
GREAT
SUPER
AMAZING

World News Today!

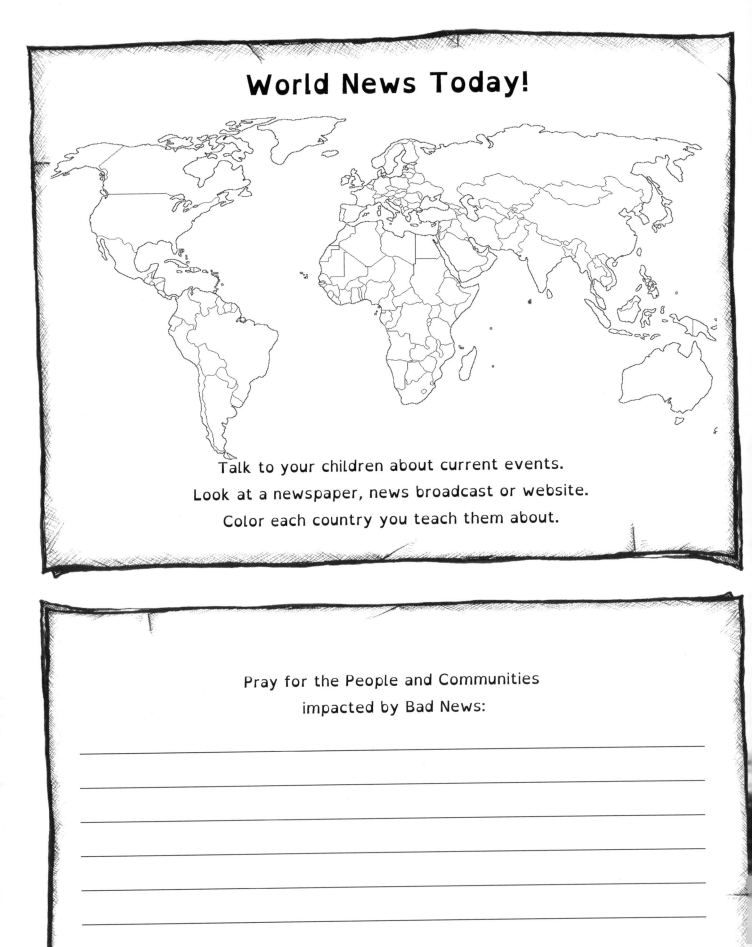

Talk to your children about current events.

Look at a newspaper, news broadcast or website.

Color each country you teach them about.

Pray for the People and Communities
impacted by Bad News:

_____

_____

_____

_____

_____

_____

Daily Journal

_____
_____
_____
_____
_____
_____
_____
_____
_____
_____
_____
_____

Special Memories

Things that you want to remember...

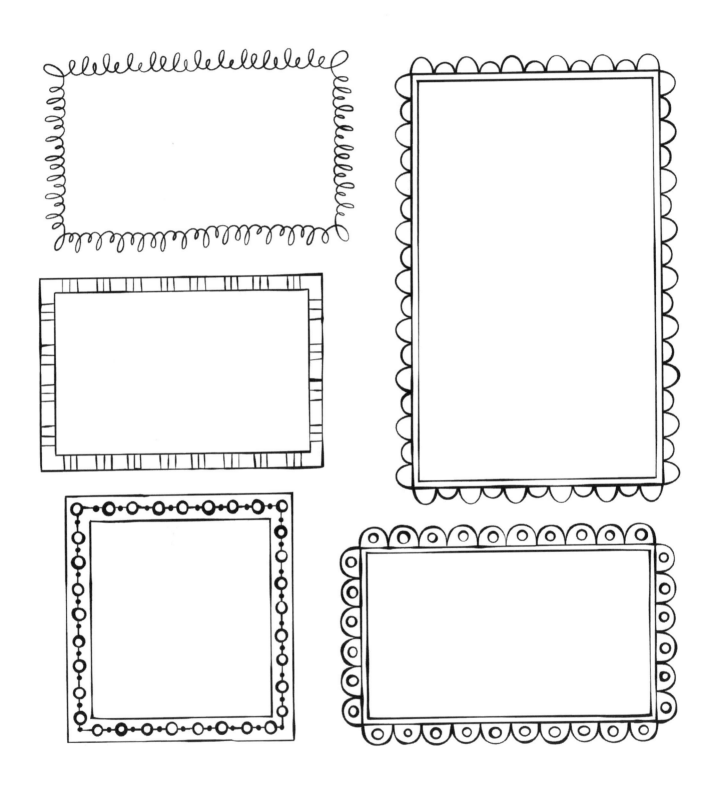

Mom's Coloring Time

Coloring beautiful pictures and doodling
relieves stress and helps with creativity & relaxation.

"The true sign of intelligence is not knowledge but imagination." ~ Albert Einstein

A New Day!

My Verse, My Song or My Prayer...

What Matters Most...

Prayer List

Plans & Perspective

"The home is the first and most effective place to learn the lessons of life: truth, honor, virtue, self control, the value of education, honest work, and the purpose and privilege of life." -McKay

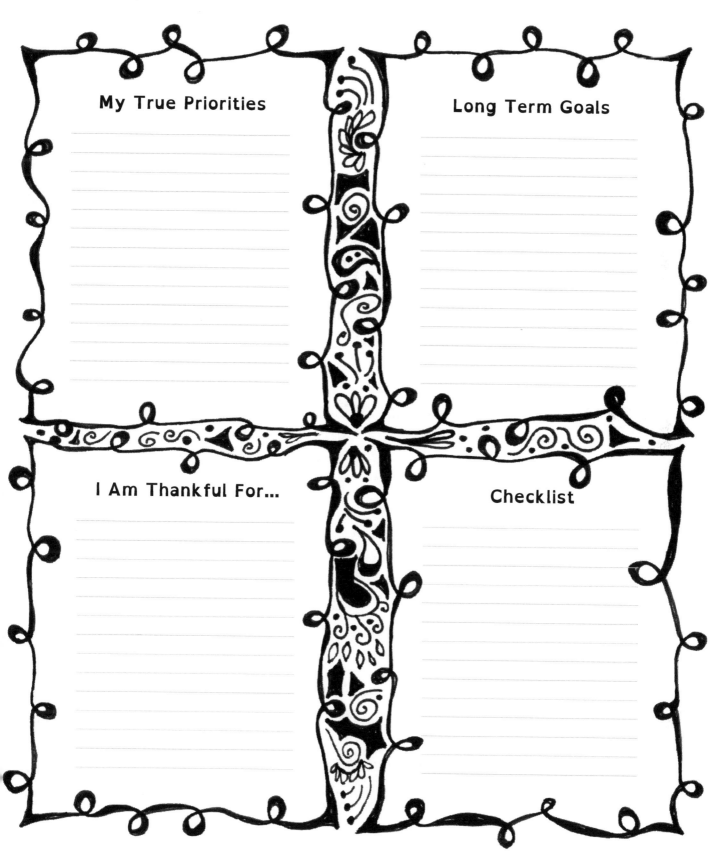

My True Priorities

Long Term Goals

I Am Thankful For...

Checklist

A Vision for Your Life

What is your vision, and what are you doing to archive it in everyday life?

_____

_____

_____

_____

Your calling and purpose is unlike any other.
Ask God for His plans for your life. Ask God for wisdom,
guidance and strength to fulfill your purpose today.

Draw a picture of your dreams for this day,
for your future, for yourself, for your home,
your marriage or for your family.

Reading Time

Sit down with a few books from your stack.

Write, draw or copy the things you want to remember.

Mom's Illustrated TO-DO List

Mom's Coloring Time

Coloring beautiful pictures and doodling
relieves stress and helps with creativity & relaxation.

Ideas for Fun & Learning Together

Menu Planning

Open up an old-fashion cookbook!

_____

_____

_____

_____

_____

_____

Shopping List

_____

_____

_____

_____

_____

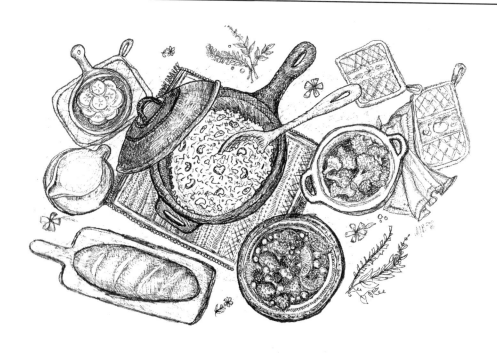

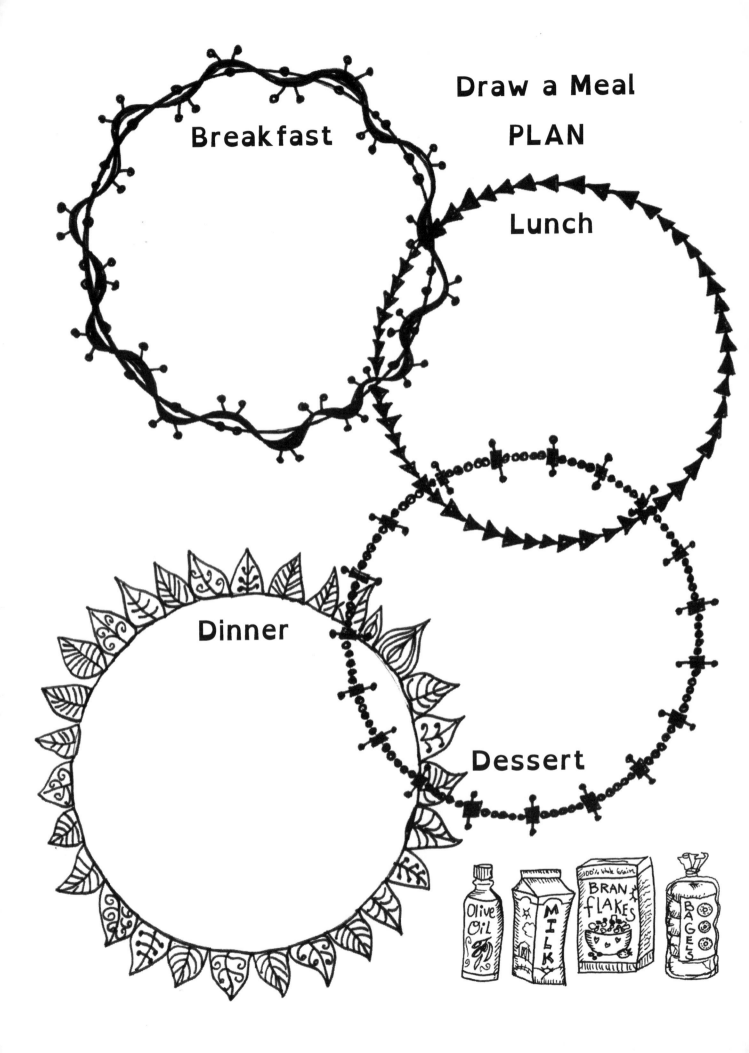

Breakfast

Draw a Meal
PLAN

Lunch

Dinner

Dessert

Recipe:

_____

Serves:

Prep Time:

Ingredients:

Instructions:

Shopping List:

"Recipe for genius: More of family and less of school, more of parents and less of peers, more creative freedom and less formal lessons." ~Raymond Moore

A New Day!

My Verse, My Song or My Prayer...

What Matters Most...

Prayer List

Mom's Coloring Time

Coloring beautiful pictures and doodling
relieves stress and helps with creativity & relaxation.

"The true sign of intelligence is not knowledge but imagination." ~ Albert Einstein

Plans & Perspective

"The home is the first and most effective place to learn the lessons of life: truth, honor, virtue, self control, the value of education, honest work, and the purpose and privilege of life." -McKay

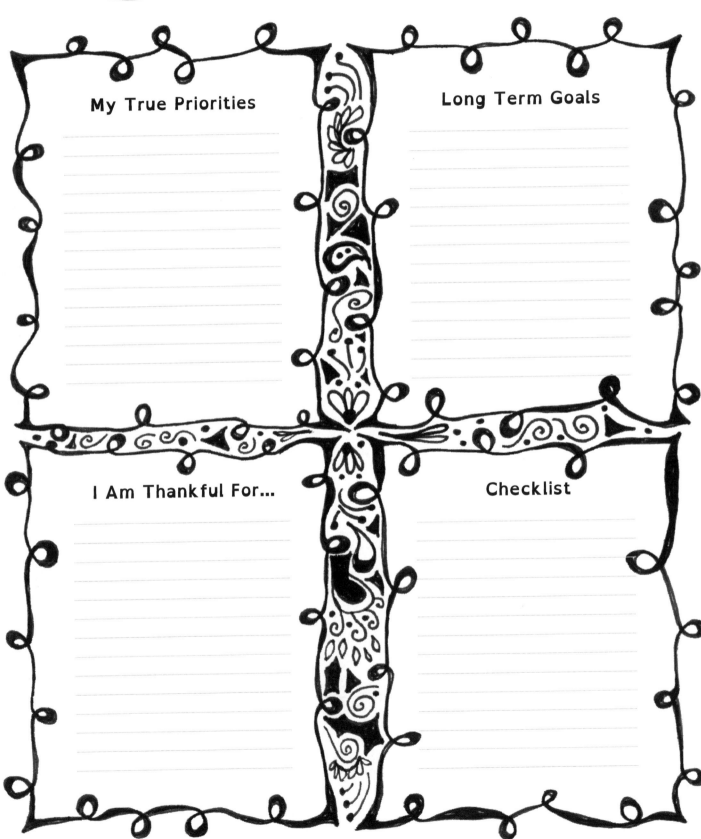

My True Priorities

Long Term Goals

I Am Thankful For...

Checklist

Reading Time

Sit down with a few books from your stack.

Write, draw or copy the things you want to remember.

A Vision for Your Life

What is your vision, and what are you doing to archive it in everyday life?

_____

_____

_____

_____

Your calling and purpose is unlike any other.
Ask God for His plans for your life. Ask God for wisdom,
guidance and strength to fulfill your purpose today.

Draw a picture of your dreams for this day,
for your future, for yourself, for your home,
your marriage or for your family.

Reading Time

Sit down with a few books from your stack.

Write, draw or copy the things you want to remember.

Mom's Illustrated TO-DO List

Ideas for Fun & Learning Together

Menu Planning

Open up an old-fashion cookbook!

_____

_____

_____

_____

_____

_____

Shopping List

_____

_____

_____

_____

_____

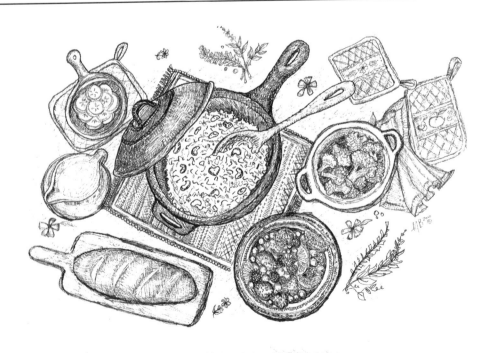

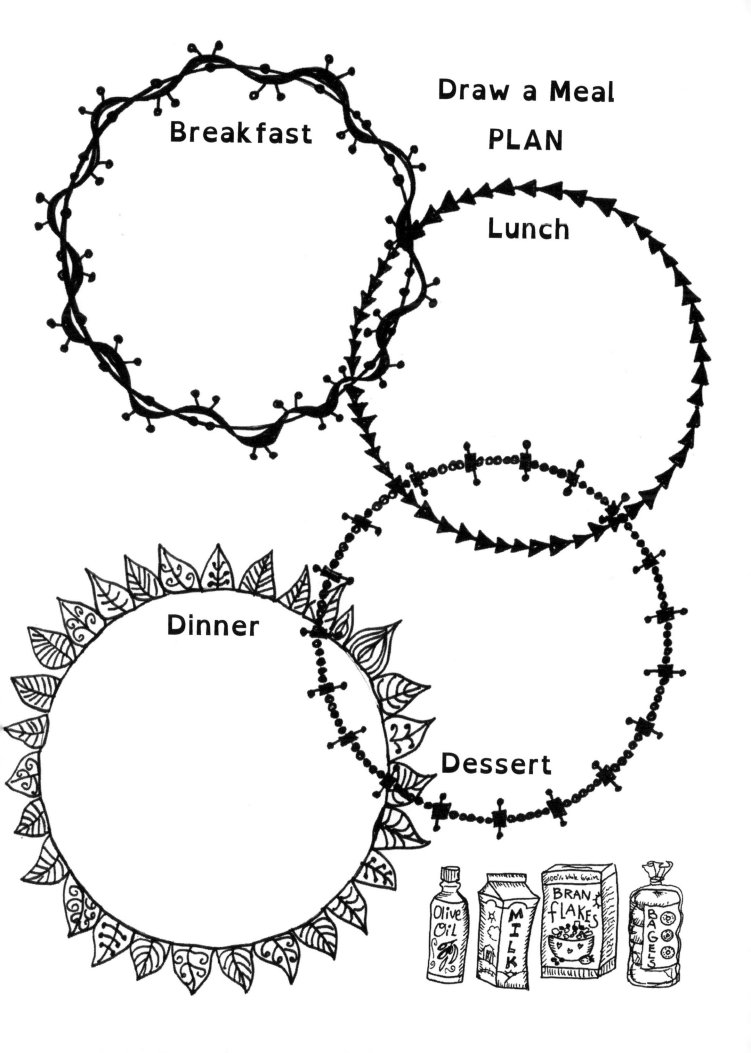

Recipe:

_____

Serves:

Prep Time:

Ingredients:

Instructions:

Shopping List:

"Recipe for genius: More of family and less of school, more of parents and less of peers,

more creative freedom and less formal lessons." ~Raymond Moore

Mommy Math Time

Math is something that Kids need help with.

Go get a kid and show them how to do some math here:

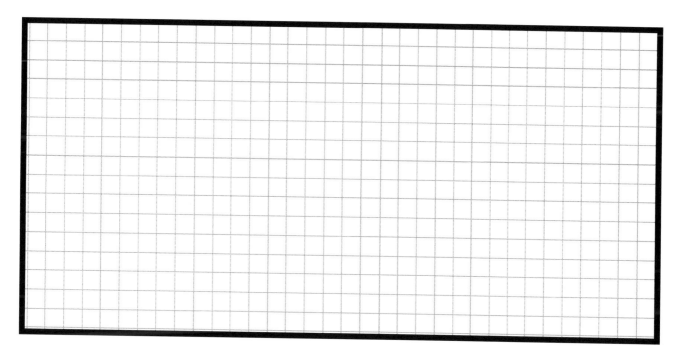

"Everything I am interested in, from cooking to electronics, is related to math. In real life you don't have to worry about integrating math into other subjects. In real life, math already is integrated into everything else." ~ Hoffstrom

Listening Time

Listen to an audio book or classical music or
ask someone to read a story to you while
you color and draw on the next page.

What are you listening to?

_____

Reading Time

Sit down with a few books from your stack.

Write, draw or copy the things you want to remember.

TITLE:

STARS:

Screen Time!

Watch a Documentary, Educational Program, Movie, or Tutorial.

My Review of this Film:

Rating:
AWFUL
BAD
LAME
YUCKY
OKAY
NICE
GOOD
GREAT
SUPER
AMAZING

Draw a Scene from the video:

World News Today!

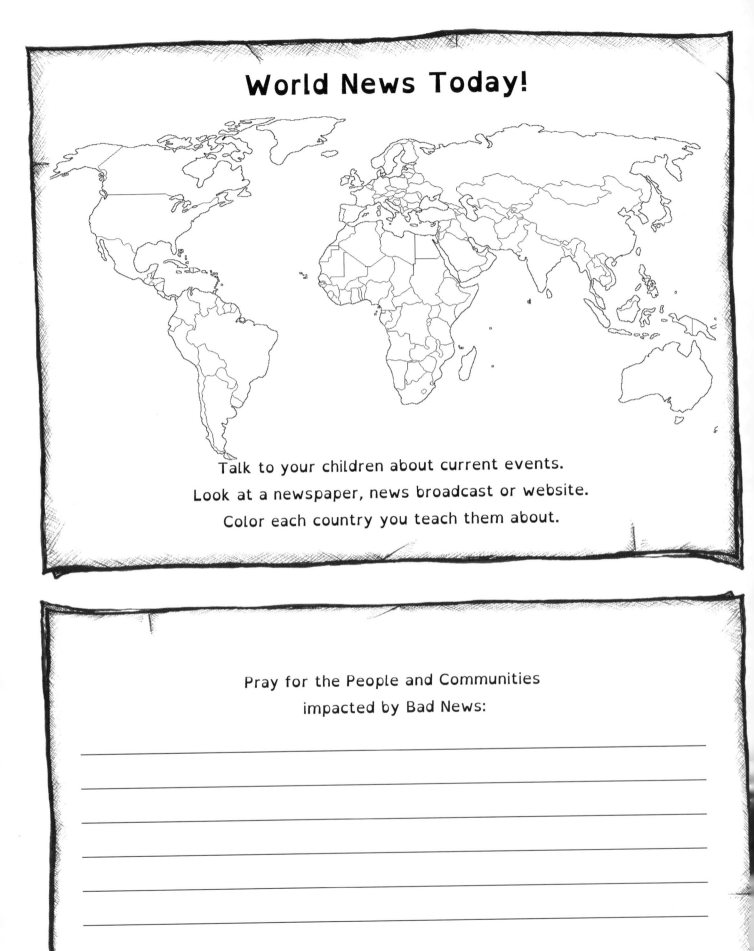

Talk to your children about current events.

Look at a newspaper, news broadcast or website.

Color each country you teach them about.

Pray for the People and Communities
impacted by Bad News:

_____

_____

_____

_____

_____

_____

Daily Journal

_____
_____
_____
_____
_____
_____
_____
_____
_____
_____
_____
_____

A New Day!

My Verse, My Song or My Prayer...

_____
_____
_____
_____
_____
_____
_____

What Matters Most...

_____
_____
_____
_____
_____
_____

Prayer List

_____
_____
_____
_____
_____
_____
_____
_____
_____

Mom's Coloring Time

Coloring beautiful pictures and doodling
relieves stress and helps with creativity & relaxation.

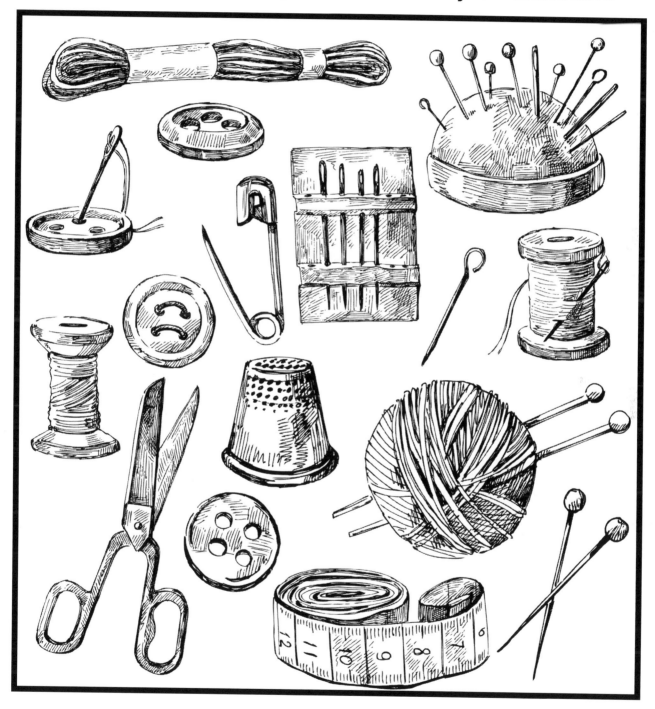

"The true sign of intelligence is not knowledge but imagination." ~ Albert Einstein

Plans & Perspective

"The home is the first and most effective place to learn the lessons of life: truth, honor, virtue, self control, the value of education, honest work, and the purpose and privilege of life." -McKay

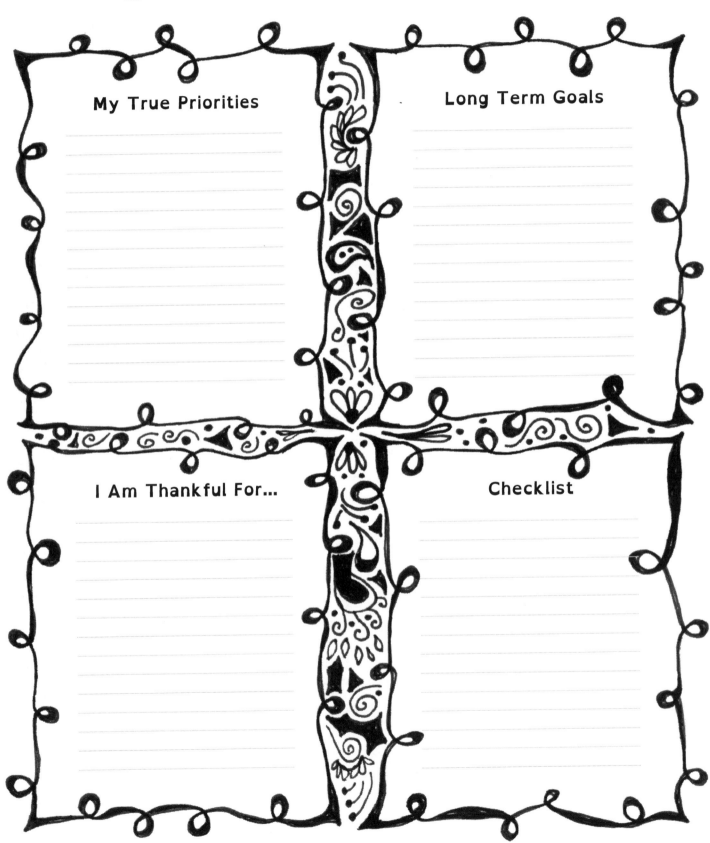

My True Priorities

Long Term Goals

I Am Thankful For...

Checklist

A Vision for Your Life

What is your vision, and what are you doing to archive it in everyday life?

_____

_____

_____

_____

Your calling and purpose is unlike any other.
Ask God for His plans for your life. Ask God for wisdom,
guidance and strength to fulfill your purpose today.

Draw a picture of your dreams for this day,
for your future, for yourself, for your home,
your marriage or for your family.

Reading Time

Sit down with a few books from your stack.

Write, draw or copy the things you want to remember.

Mom's Illustrated TO-DO List

Ideas for Fun & Learning Together

Menu Planning

Open up an old-fashion cookbook!

_____

_____

_____

_____

_____

_____

Shopping List

_____

_____

_____

_____

_____

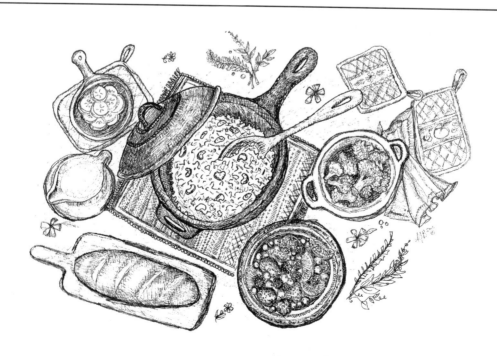

A New Day!

My Verse, My Song or My Prayer...

_____
_____
_____
_____
_____
_____
_____
_____

What Matters Most...

_____
_____
_____
_____
_____
_____

Prayer List

_____
_____
_____
_____
_____
_____
_____
_____

Mom's Coloring Time

Coloring beautiful pictures and doodling
relieves stress and helps with creativity & relaxation.

"The true sign of intelligence is not knowledge but imagination." ~ Albert Einstein

Plans & Perspective

"The home is the first and most effective place to learn the lessons of life: truth, honor, virtue, self control, the value of education, honest work, and the purpose and privilege of life." -McKay

My True Priorities

Long Term Goals

I Am Thankful For...

Checklist

A Vision for Your Life

What is your vision, and what are you doing to archive it in everyday life?

_____

_____

_____

_____

Your calling and purpose is unlike any other.
Ask God for His plans for your life. Ask God for wisdom,
guidance and strength to fulfill your purpose today.

Draw a picture of your dreams for this day,
for your future, for yourself, for your home,
your marriage or for your family.

Reading Time

Sit down with a few books from your stack.

Write, draw or copy the things you want to remember.

Mom's Illustrated TO-DO List

Mom's Coloring Time

Coloring beautiful pictures and doodling
relieves stress and helps with creativity & relaxation.

Reading Time

Sit down with a few books from your stack.

Write, draw or copy the things you want to remember.

Ideas for Fun & Learning Together

Menu Planning

Open up an old-fashion cookbook!

_____

_____

_____

_____

_____

_____

Shopping List

_____

_____

_____

_____

_____

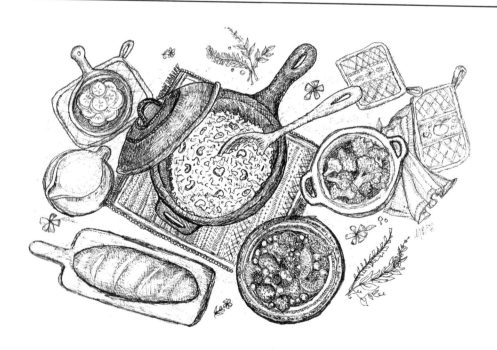

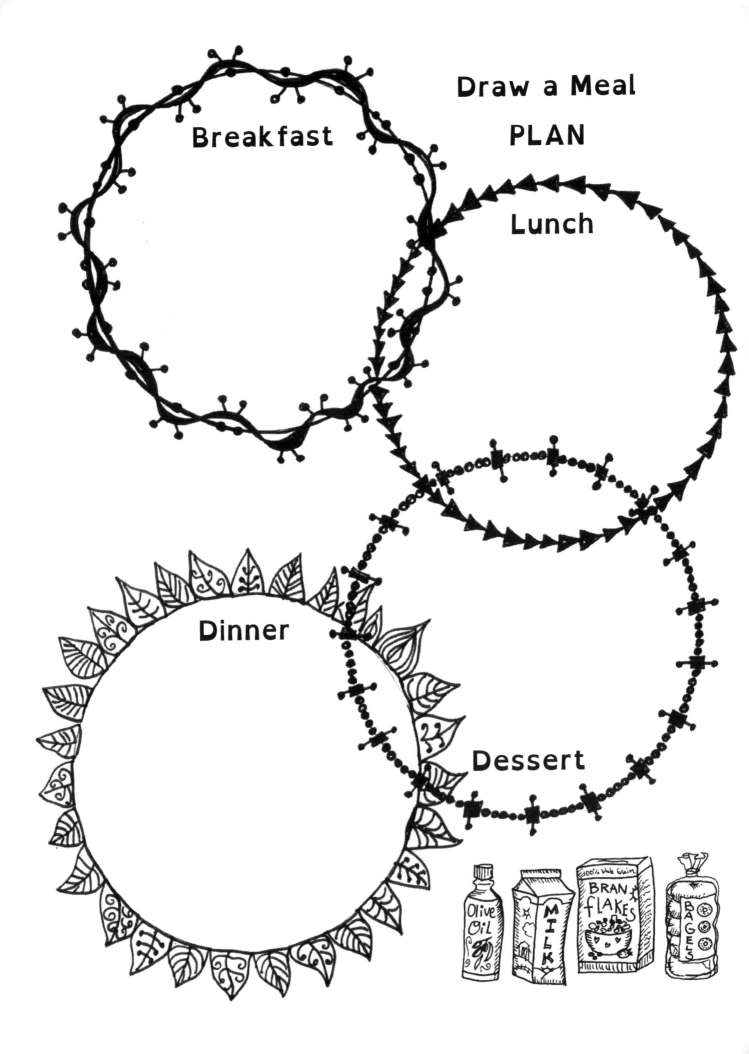

Breakfast

Draw a Meal
PLAN

Lunch

Dinner

Dessert

Recipe:

_____

Serves:

Prep Time:

Ingredients:

Instructions:

Shopping List:

"Recipe for genius: More of family and less of school, more of parents and less of peers, more creative freedom and less formal lessons." ~Raymond Moore

Mommy Math Time

Math is something that Kids need help with.

Go get a kid and show them how to do some math here:

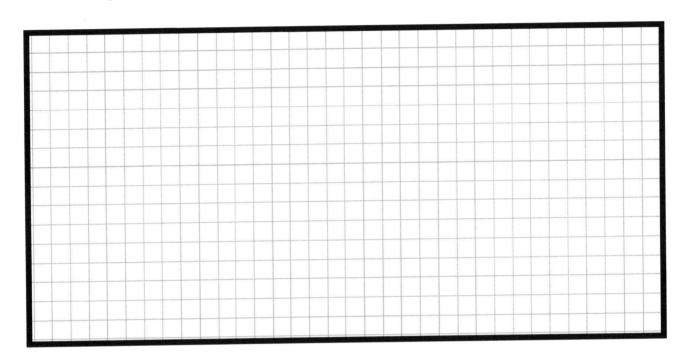

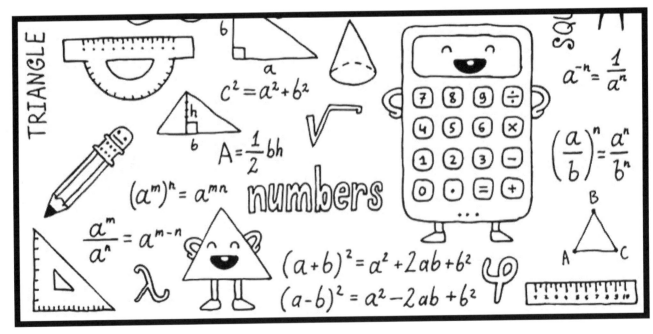

"Everything I am interested in, from cooking to electronics, is related to math. In real life you don't have to worry about integrating math into other subjects. In real life, math already is integrated into everything else." ~ Hoffstrom

Listening Time

Listen to an audio book or classical music or
ask someone to read a story to you while
you color and draw on the next page.

What are you listening to?

_____

TITLE:

STARS:

Screen Time!

Watch a Documentary, Educational Program, Movie, or Tutorial.

My Review of this Film:

Draw a Scene from the video:

Rating:
AWFUL
BAD
LAME
YUCKY
OKAY
NICE
GOOD
GREAT
SUPER
AMAZING

What song do you want to sing today?

Write a few verses here:

Mom's Coloring Time

Coloring beautiful pictures and doodling
relieves stress and helps with creativity & relaxation.

World News Today!

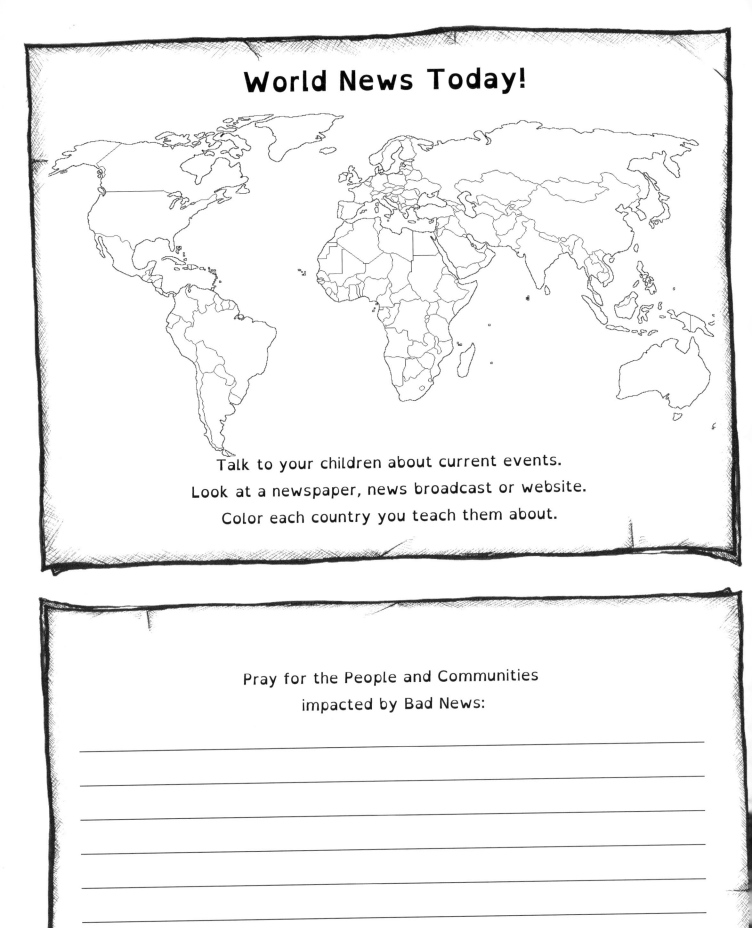

Talk to your children about current events.

Look at a newspaper, news broadcast or website.

Color each country you teach them about.

Pray for the People and Communities
impacted by Bad News:

_____

_____

_____

_____

_____

_____

Reading Time

Sit down with a few books from your stack.

Write, draw or copy the things you want to remember.

Daily Journal

_____

_____

_____

_____

_____

_____

_____

_____

_____

_____

_____

"Education is not filling a bucket,
but lighting a fire." ~W.B. Yeats

A New Day!

My Verse, My Song or My Prayer...

What Matters Most...

Prayer List

Mom's Coloring Time

Coloring beautiful pictures and doodling
relieves stress and helps with creativity & relaxation.

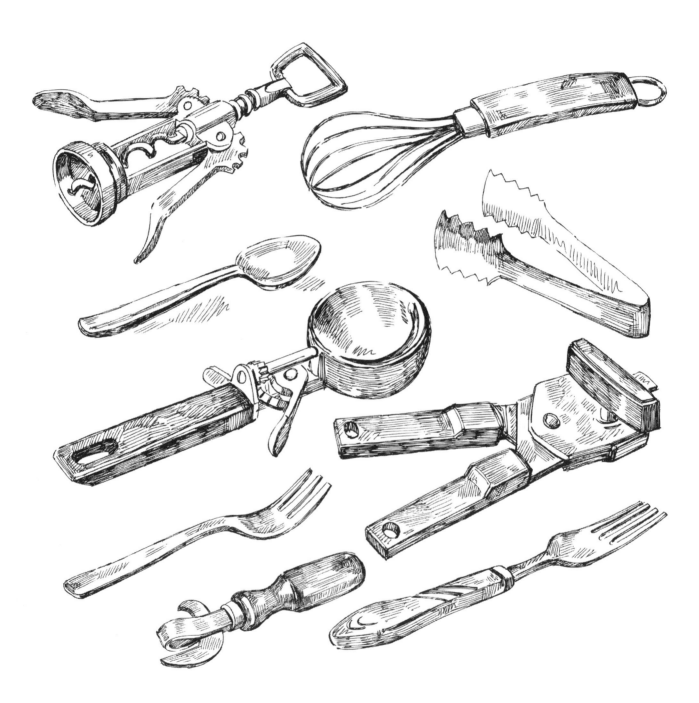

"The true sign of intelligence is not knowledge but imagination." ~ Albert Einstein

Plans & Perspective

"The home is the first and most effective place to learn the lessons of life: truth, honor, virtue, self control, the value of education, honest work, and the purpose and privilege of life." -McKay

My True Priorities

Long Term Goals

I Am Thankful For...

Checklist

A Vision for Your Life

What is your vision, and what are you doing to archive it in everyday life?

_____

_____

_____

_____

Your calling and purpose is unlike any other.
Ask God for His plans for your life. Ask God for wisdom,
guidance and strength to fulfill your purpose today.

Draw a picture of your dreams for this day,
for your future, for yourself, for your home,
your marriage or for your family.

Reading Time

Sit down with a few books from your stack.

Write, draw or copy the things you want to remember.

Mom's Coloring Time

Coloring beautiful pictures and doodling
relieves stress and helps with creativity & relaxation.

Mom's Illustrated TO-DO List

Ideas for Fun & Learning Together

Menu Planning

Open up an old-fashion cookbook!

_____

_____

_____

_____

_____

_____

Shopping List

_____

_____

_____

_____

_____

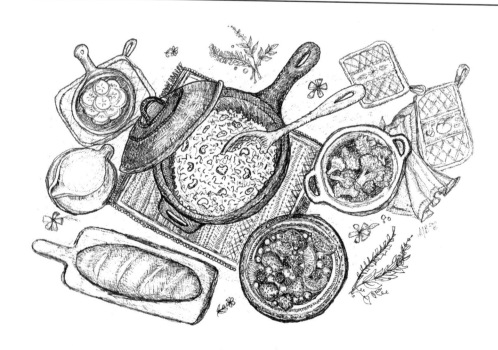

Reading Time

Sit down with a few books from your stack.

Write, draw or copy the things you want to remember.

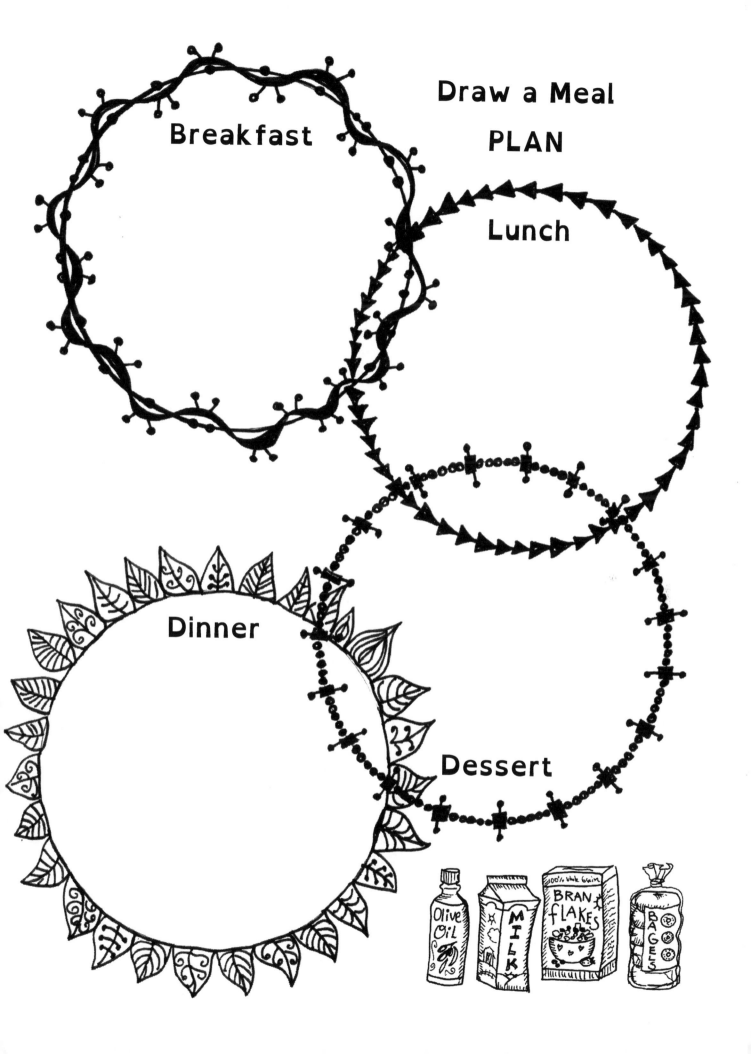

Recipe:

_____

Serves:

Prep Time:

Ingredients:

Instructions:

- In a bowl, combine the banana, eggs and cinnamon.
- Mix/mash until the mixture becomes all smooth. You can use a fork or a potato masher to achieve that.
- Grease your pan with a little bit of oil or butter.
- Heat your stove to a low to medium setting.
- Pour ¼ of the batter in your pan and cook for about 1½ minutes on both sides.
- Serve as is or garnish with anything you like banana slices with cinnamon and honey.

Shopping List:

"Recipe for genius: More of family and less of school, more of parents and less of peers, more creative freedom and less formal lessons." ~Raymond Moore

Mommy Math Time

Math is something that Kids need help with.
Go get a kid and show them how to do some math here:

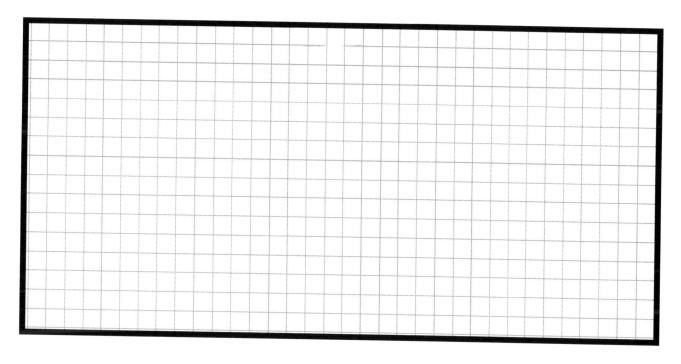

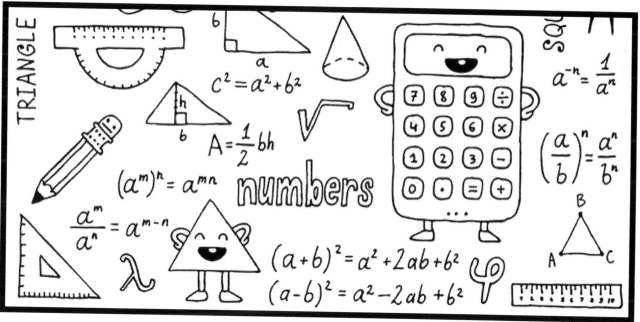

"Everything I am interested in, from cooking to electronics, is related to math. In real life you don't have to worry about integrating math into other subjects. In real life, math already is integrated into everything else." ~ Hoffstrom

Listening Time

Listen to an audio book or classical music or
ask someone to read a story to you while
you color and draw on the next page.

What are you listening to?

_____

TITLE:

STARS:

Screen Time!

Watch a Documentary, Educational Program, Movie, or Tutorial.

My Review of this Film:

Rating:
AWFUL
BAD
LAME
YUCKY
OKAY
NICE
GOOD
GREAT
SUPER
AMAZING

Draw a Scene from the video:

World News Today!

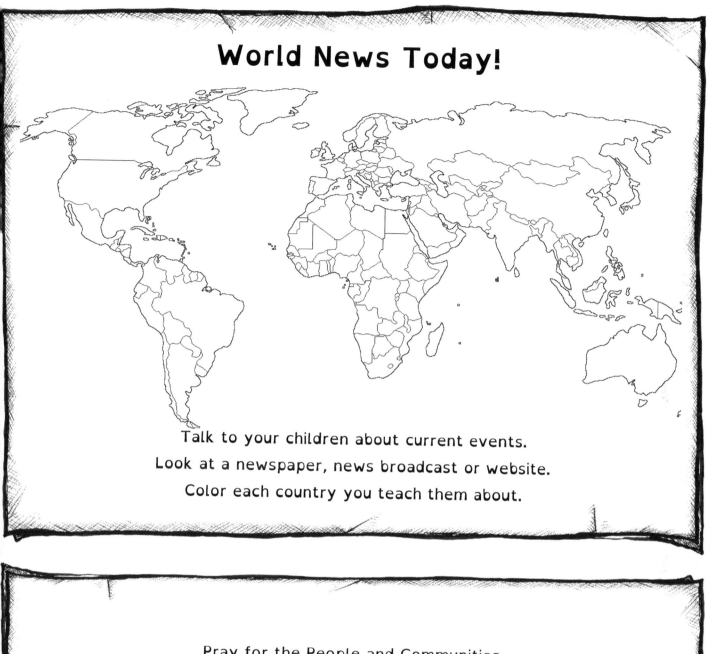

Talk to your children about current events.

Look at a newspaper, news broadcast or website.

Color each country you teach them about.

Pray for the People and Communities
impacted by Bad News:

_____

_____

_____

_____

_____

_____

Daily Journal

_____
_____
_____
_____
_____
_____
_____
_____
_____
_____
_____
_____

"Education is not filling a bucket,
but lighting a fire." ~W.B. Yeats

A New Day!

My Verse, My Song or My Prayer...

_____
_____
_____
_____
_____
_____
_____

What Matters Most...

_____
_____
_____
_____
_____

Prayer List

_____
_____
_____
_____
_____
_____
_____

Reading Time

Sit down with a few books from your stack.

Write, draw or copy the things you want to remember.

Mom's Coloring Time

Coloring beautiful pictures and doodling
relieves stress and helps with creativity & relaxation.

Plans & Perspective

"The home is the first and most effective place to learn the lessons of life: truth, honor, virtue, self control, the value of education, honest work, and the purpose and privilege of life." -McKay

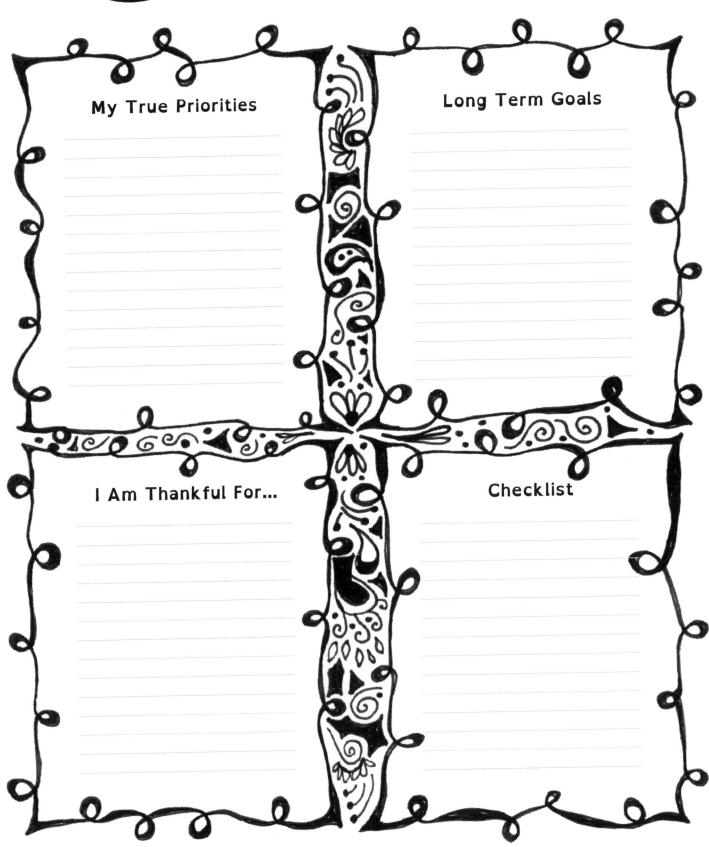

My True Priorities

Long Term Goals

I Am Thankful For...

Checklist

A Vision for Your Life

What is your vision, and what are you doing to archive it in everyday life?

_____

_____

_____

_____

Your calling and purpose is unlike any other.
Ask God for His plans for your life. Ask God for wisdom,
guidance and strength to fulfill your purpose today.

Draw a picture of your dreams for this day,
for your future, for yourself, for your home,
your marriage or for your family.

Mom's Coloring Time

Coloring beautiful pictures and doodling
relieves stress and helps with creativity & relaxation.

Reading Time

Sit down with a few books from your stack.

Write, draw or copy the things you want to remember.

What song do you want to sing today?

Write a few verses here:

Mom's Illustrated TO-DO List

Ideas for Fun & Learning Together

Mom's Coloring Time

Coloring beautiful pictures and doodling
relieves stress and helps with creativity & relaxation.

"The true sign of intelligence is not knowledge but imagination." ~ Albert Einstein

Menu Planning

Open up an old-fashion cookbook!

_____

_____

_____

_____

_____

_____

Shopping List

_____

_____

_____

_____

_____

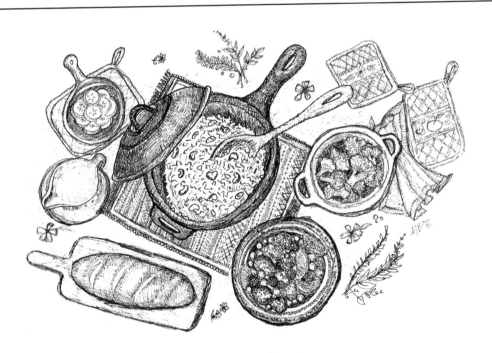

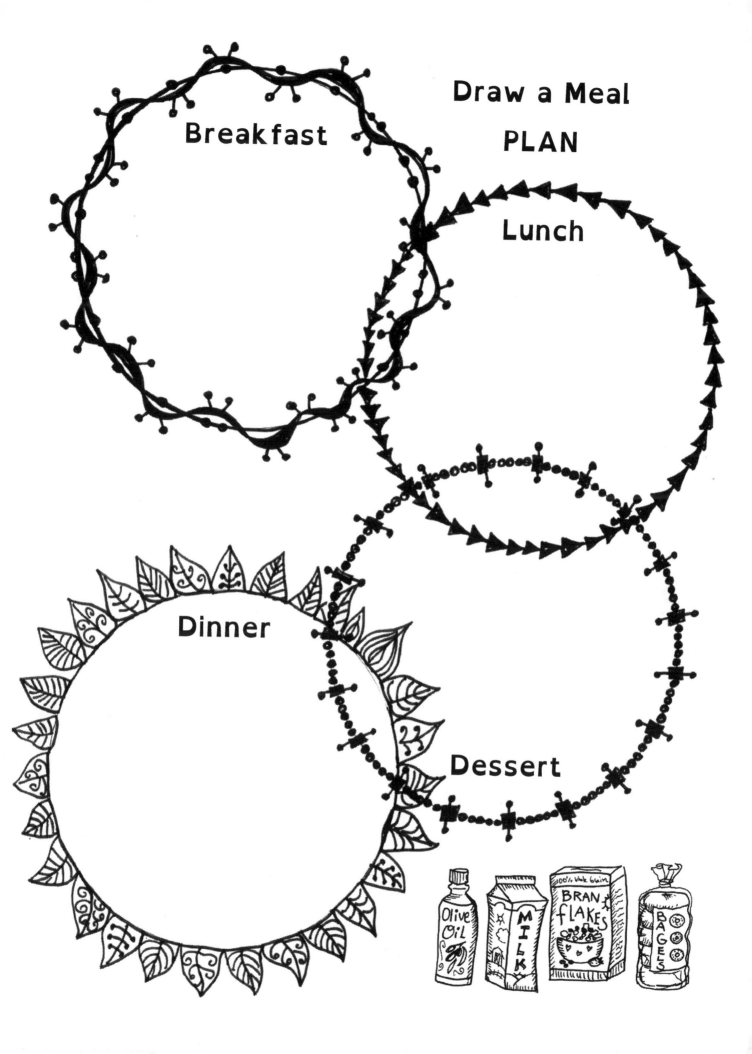

Recipe:

_____

Serves:

Prep Time:

Ingredients:

Instructions:

Shopping List:

"Recipe for genius: More of family and less of school, more of parents and less of peers, more creative freedom and less formal lessons." ~Raymond Moore

Reading Time

Sit down with a few books from your stack.

Write, draw or copy the things you want to remember.

Mommy Math Time

Math is something that Kids need help with.

Go get a kid and show them how to do some math here:

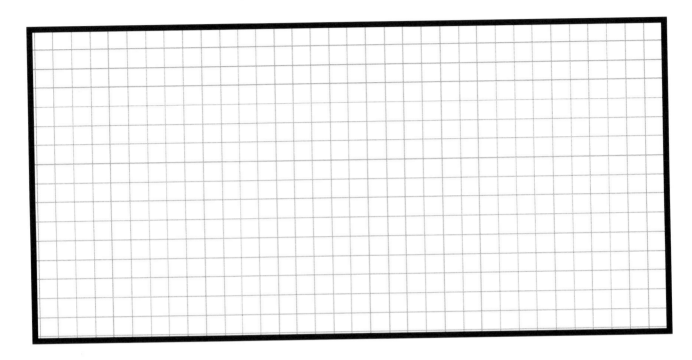

"Everything I am interested in, from cooking to electronics, is related to math. In real life you don't have to worry about integrating math into other subjects. In real life, math already is integrated into everything else." ~ Hoffstrom

Listening Time

Listen to an audio book or classical music or ask someone to read a story to you while you color and draw on the next page.

What are you listening to?

_____

TITLE:

STARS:

Screen Time!

Watch a Documentary, Educational Program, Movie, or Tutorial.

My Review of this Film:

Rating:

AWFUL

BAD

LAME

YUCKY

OKAY

NICE

GOOD

GREAT

SUPER

AMAZING

Draw a Scene from the video:

World News Today!

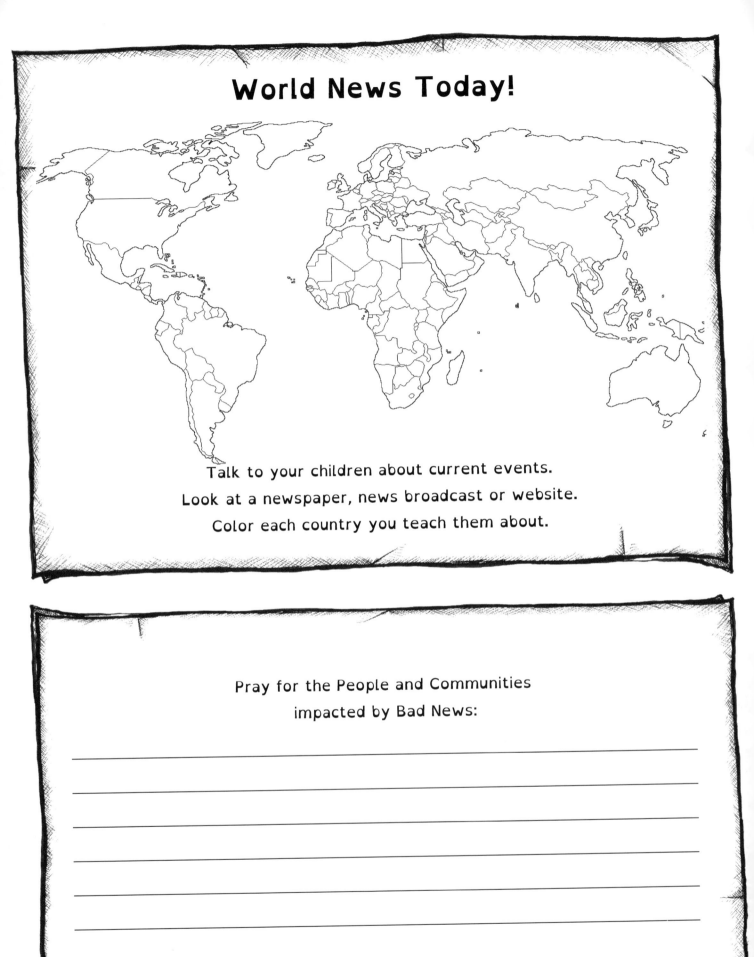

Talk to your children about current events.

Look at a newspaper, news broadcast or website.

Color each country you teach them about.

Pray for the People and Communities
impacted by Bad News:

_____

_____

_____

_____

_____

_____

Daily Journal

_____

_____

_____

_____

_____

_____

_____

_____

_____

_____

_____

_____

"Education is not filling a bucket,
but lighting a fire." ~W.B. Yeats

Special Memories

Things that you want to remember...

A New Day!

My Verse, My Song or My Prayer...

What Matters Most...

Prayer List

Reading Time

Sit down with a few books from your stack.

Write, draw or copy the things you want to remember.

Plans & Perspective

"The home is the first and most effective place to learn the lessons of life: truth, honor, virtue, self control, the value of education, honest work, and the purpose and privilege of life." -McKay

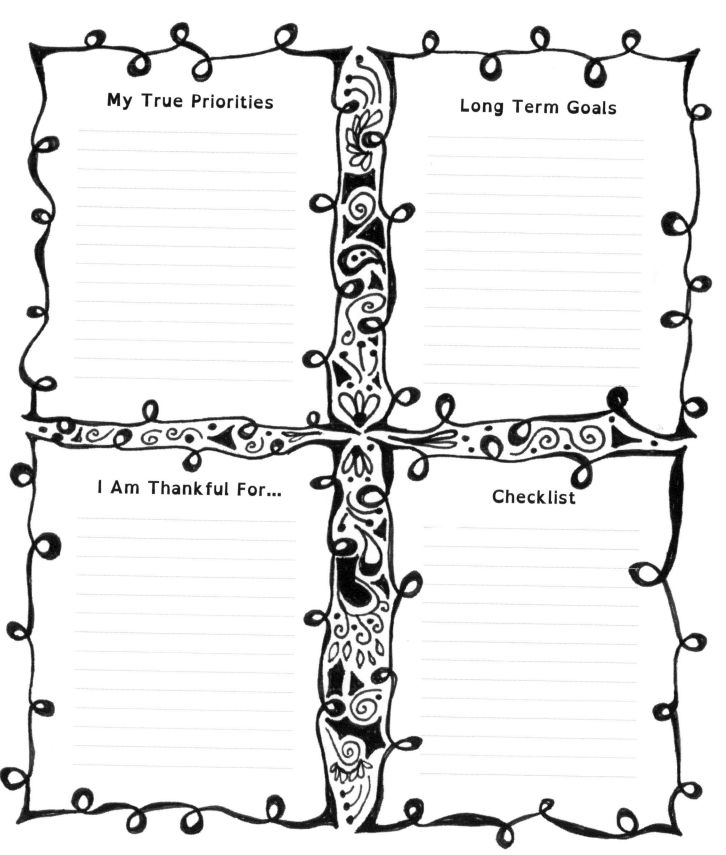

My True Priorities

Long Term Goals

I Am Thankful For...

Checklist

Mom's Coloring Time

Coloring beautiful pictures and doodling

relieves stress and helps with creativity & relaxation.

"The true sign of intelligence is not knowledge but imagination." ~ Albert Einstein

Plans & Perspective

"The home is the first and most effective place to learn the lessons of life: truth, honor, virtue, self control, the value of education, honest work, and the purpose and privilege of life." -McKay

My True Priorities

Long Term Goals

I Am Thankful For...

Checklist

A Vision for Your Life

What is your vision, and what are you doing to archive it in everyday life?

_____

_____

_____

_____

Your calling and purpose is unlike any other.
Ask God for His plans for your life. Ask God for wisdom,
guidance and strength to fulfill your purpose today.

Draw a picture of your dreams for this day,
for your future, for yourself, for your home,
your marriage or for your family.

Reading Time

Sit down with a few books from your stack.

Write, draw or copy the things you want to remember.

What song do you want to sing today?

Write a few verses here:

Mom's Coloring Time

Coloring beautiful pictures and doodling
relieves stress and helps with creativity & relaxation.

Mom's Illustrated TO-DO List

Mom's Coloring Time

Coloring beautiful pictures and doodling
relieves stress and helps with creativity & relaxation.

Ideas for Fun & Learning Together

Menu Planning

Open up an old-fashion cookbook!

_____

_____

_____

_____

_____

_____

Shopping List

_____

_____

_____

_____

_____

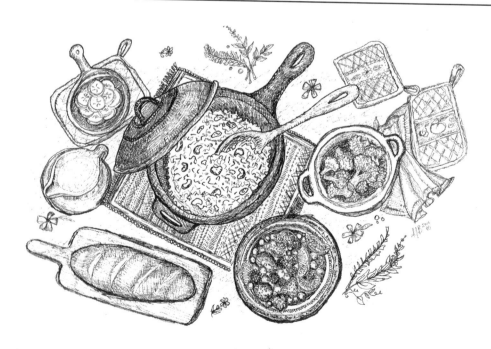

Reading Time

Sit down with a few books from your stack.

Write, draw or copy the things you want to remember.

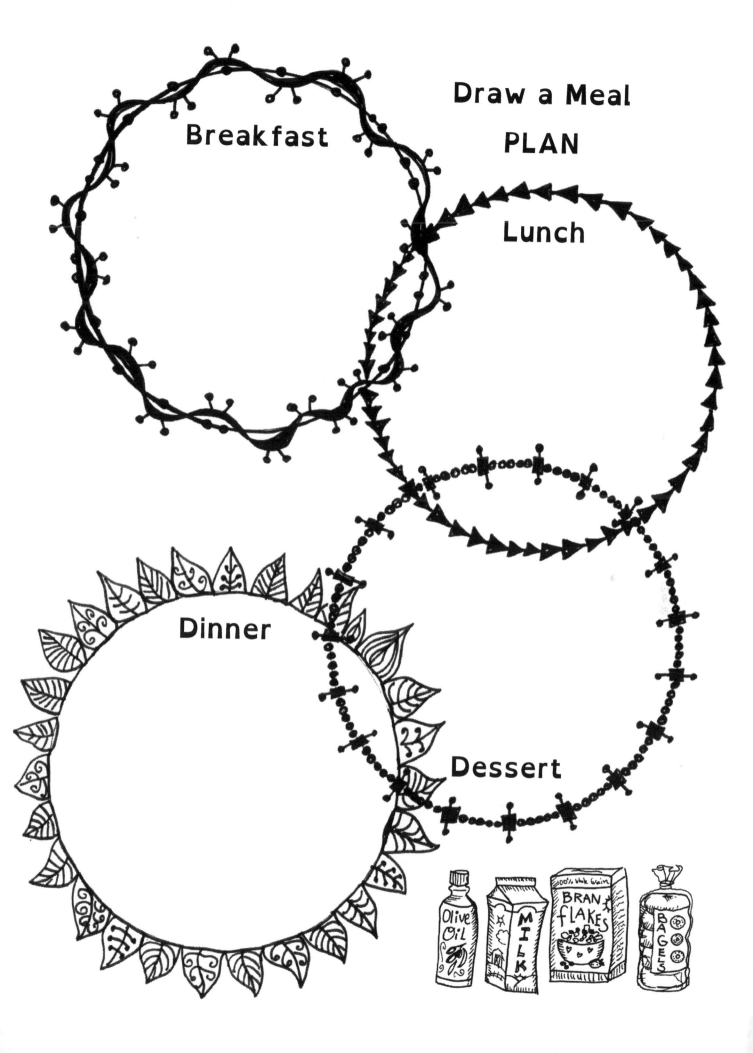

Breakfast

Draw a Meal
PLAN

Lunch

Dinner

Dessert

Recipe:

_____

Serves:

Prep Time:

Ingredients:

Instructions:

Shopping List:

"Recipe for genius: More of family and less of school, more of parents and less of peers, more creative freedom and less formal lessons."   ~Raymond Moore

Mommy Math Time

Math is something that Kids need help with.
Go get a kid and show them how to do some math here:

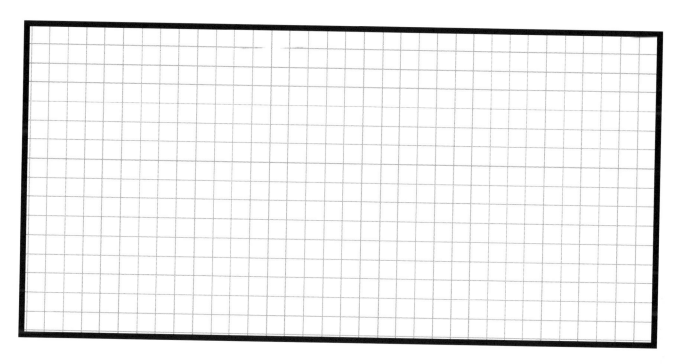

"Everything I am interested in, from cooking to electronics, is related to math. In real life you don't have to worry about integrating math into other subjects. In real life, math already is integrated into everything else." ~ Hoffstrom

Listening Time

Listen to an audio book or classical music or ask someone to read a story to you while you color and draw on the next page.

What are you listening to?

_____

TITLE:

STARS:

Screen Time!
Watch a Documentary, Educational Program, Movie, or Tutorial.

My Review of this Film:

Rating:
AWFUL
BAD
LAME
YUCKY
OKAY
NICE
GOOD
GREAT
SUPER
AMAZING

Draw a Scene from the video:

World News Today!

Talk to your children about current events.
Look at a newspaper, news broadcast or website.
Color each country you teach them about.

Pray for the People and Communities
impacted by Bad News:

_____

_____

_____

_____

_____

_____

Mom's Coloring Time

Coloring beautiful pictures and doodling
relieves stress and helps with creativity & relaxation.

Daily Journal

_____

_____

_____

_____

_____

_____

_____

_____

_____

_____

_____

_____

"Education is not filling a bucket,
but lighting a fire." ~W.B. Yeats

Special Memories

Things that you want to remember...

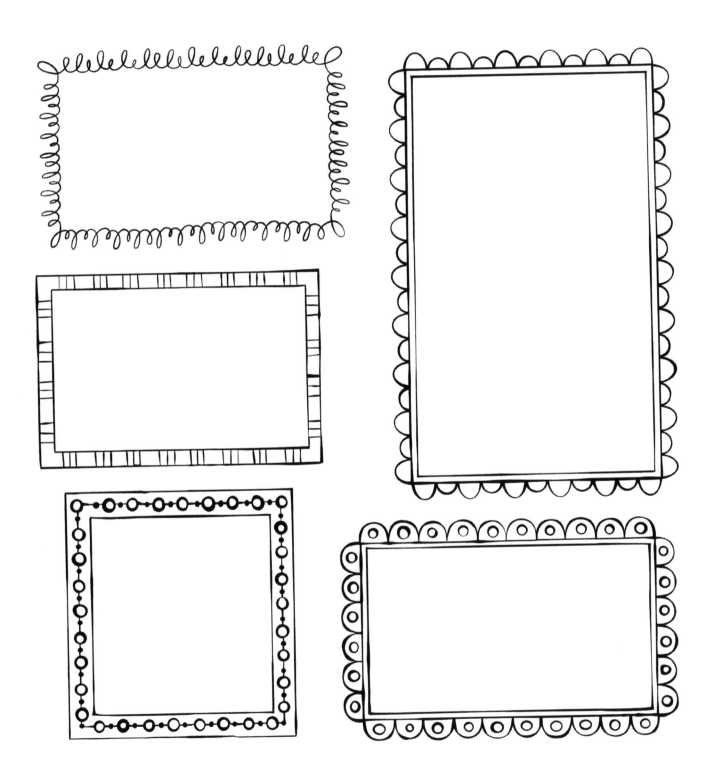

Reading Time

Sit down with a few books from your stack.
Write, draw or copy the things you want to remember.

A New Day!

My Verse, My Song or My Prayer...

What Matters Most...

Prayer List

Mom's Coloring Time

Coloring beautiful pictures and doodling
relieves stress and helps with creativity & relaxation.

"The true sign of intelligence is not knowledge but imagination." ~ Albert Einstein

Plans & Perspective

"The home is the first and most effective place to learn the lessons of life: truth, honor, virtue, self control, the value of education, honest work, and the purpose and privilege of life." -McKay

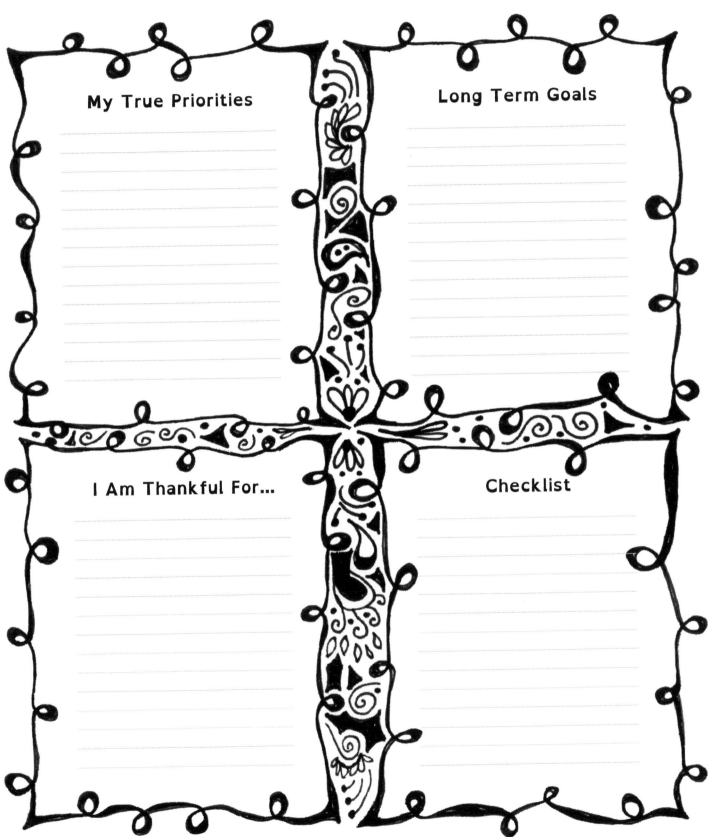

My True Priorities

Long Term Goals

I Am Thankful For...

Checklist

A New Day!

My Verse, My Song or My Prayer...

What Matters Most...

Prayer List

Mom's Coloring Time

Coloring beautiful pictures and doodling
relieves stress and helps with creativity & relaxation.

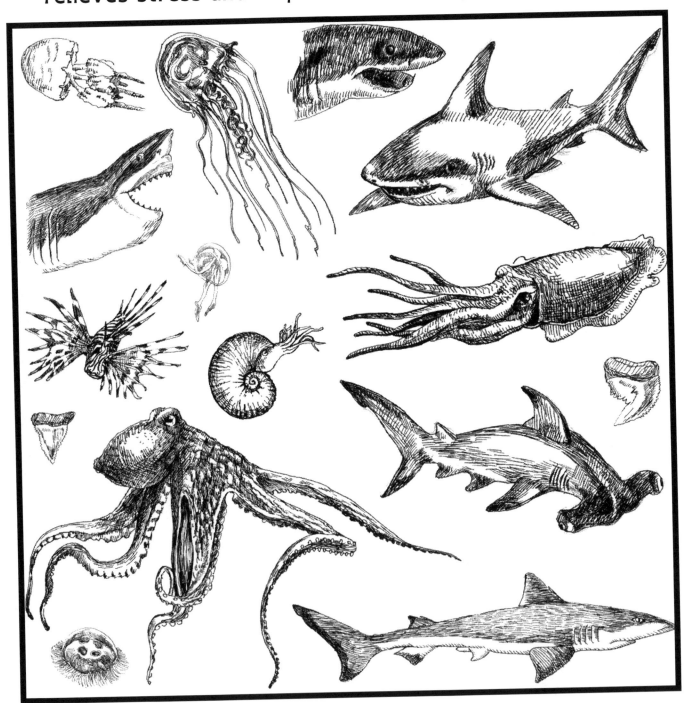

"The true sign of intelligence is not knowledge but imagination." ~ Albert Einstein

Plans & Perspective

"The home is the first and most effective place to learn the lessons of life: truth, honor, virtue, self control, the value of education, honest work, and the purpose and privilege of life." -McKay

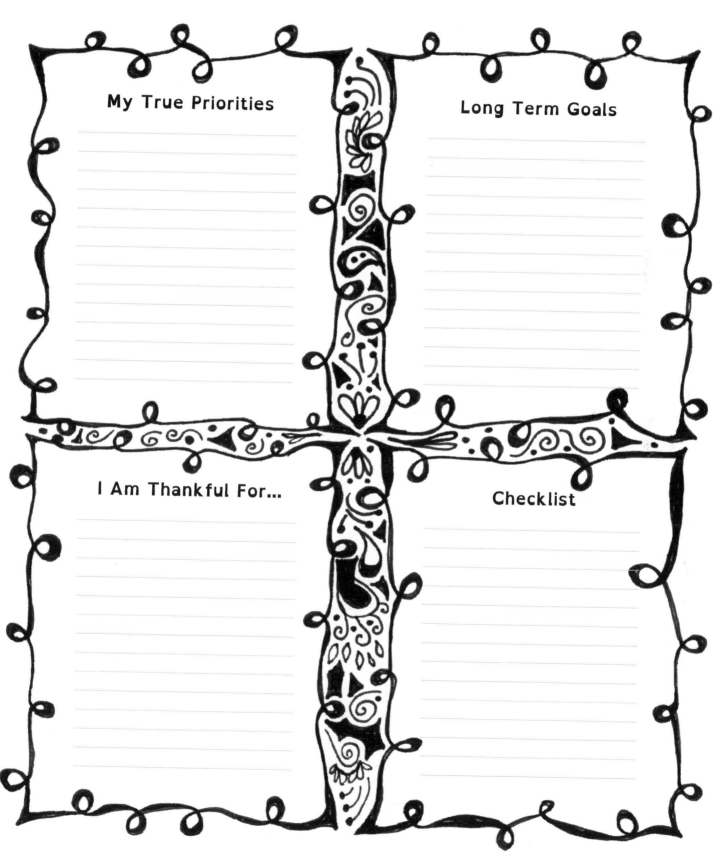

My True Priorities

Long Term Goals

I Am Thankful For...

Checklist

A Vision for Your Life

What is your vision, and what are you doing to archive it in everyday life?

_____

_____

_____

_____

Your calling and purpose is unlike any other.
Ask God for His plans for your life. Ask God for wisdom,
guidance and strength to fulfill your purpose today.

Draw a picture of your dreams for this day,
for your future, for yourself, for your home,
your marriage or for your family.

Reading Time

Sit down with a few books from your stack.

Write, draw or copy the things you want to remember.

Mom's Illustrated TO-DO List

Reading Time

Sit down with a few books from your stack.

Write, draw or copy the things you want to remember.

Ideas for Fun & Learning Together

Menu Planning

Open up an old-fashion cookbook!

_____

_____

_____

_____

_____

_____

Shopping List

_____

_____

_____

_____

_____

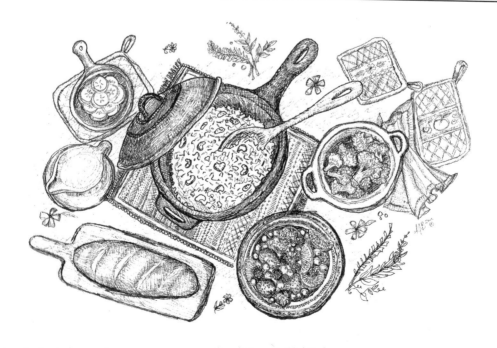

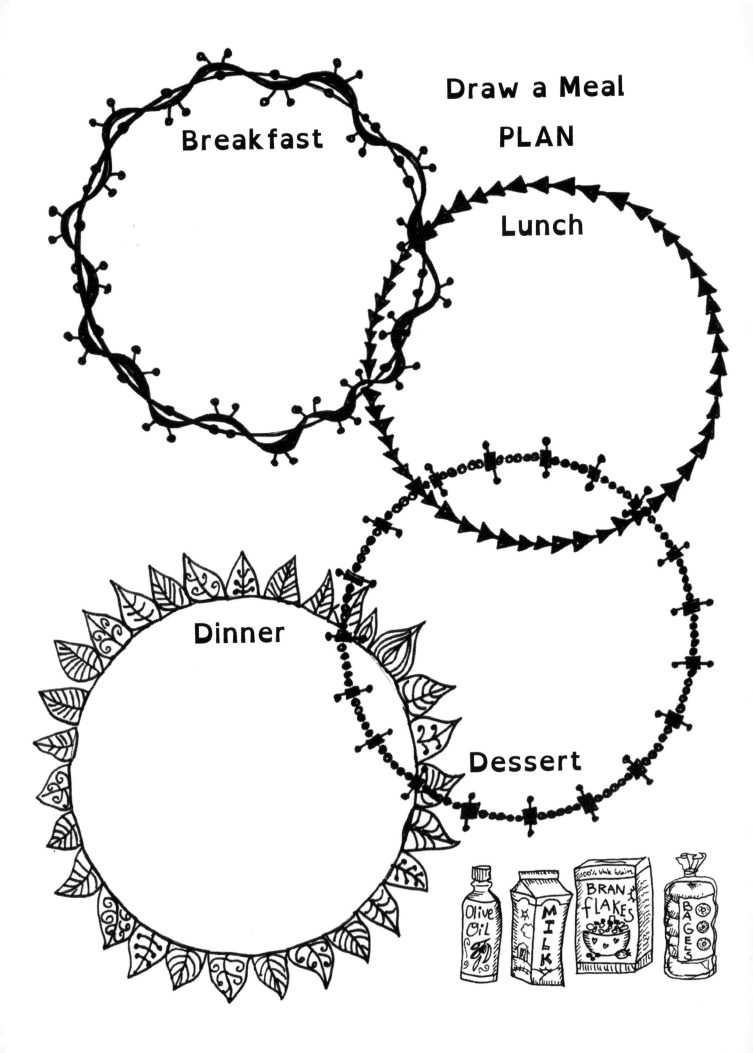

Draw a Meal
PLAN

Breakfast

Lunch

Dinner

Dessert

Recipe:

_____

Serves:

Prep Time:

Ingredients:

Instructions:

Shopping List:

"Recipe for genius: More of family and less of school, more of parents and less of peers, more creative freedom and less formal lessons." ~Raymond Moore

What song do you want to sing today?

Write a few verses here:

Mommy Math Time

Math is something that Kids need help with.
Go get a kid and show them how to do some math here:

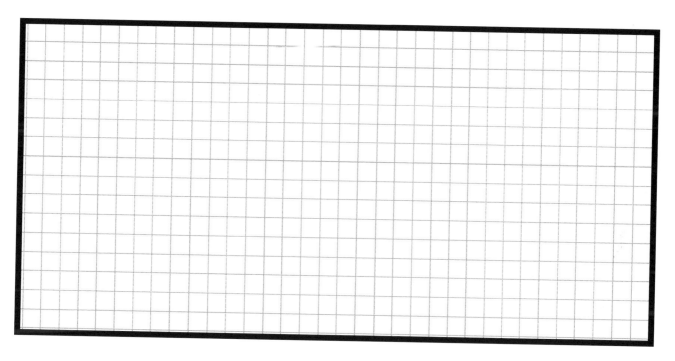

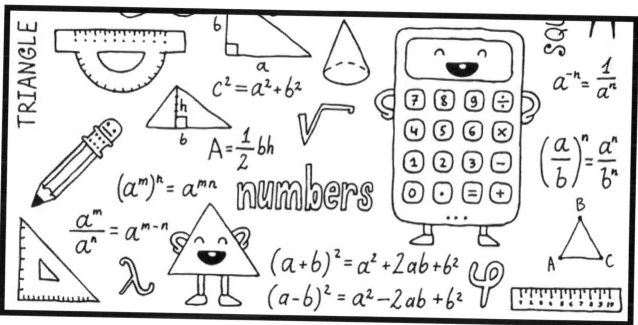

"Everything I am interested in, from cooking to electronics, is related to math. In real life you don't have to worry about integrating math into other subjects. In real life, math already is integrated into everything else." ~ Hoffstrom

Listening Time

Listen to an audio book or classical music or
ask someone to read a story to you while
you color and draw on the next page.

What are you listening to?

_____

TITLE:

STARS:

Screen Time!

Watch a Documentary, Educational Program, Movie, or Tutorial.

My Review of this Film:

Draw a Scene from the video:

Rating:
AWFUL
BAD
LAME
YUCKY
OKAY
NICE
GOOD
GREAT
SUPER
AMAZING

World News Today!

Talk to your children about current events.

Look at a newspaper, news broadcast or website.

Color each country you teach them about.

Pray for the People and Communities
impacted by Bad News:

_____

_____

_____

_____

_____

_____

Daily Journal

_____
_____
_____
_____
_____
_____
_____
_____
_____
_____
_____
_____

"Education is not filling a bucket,
but lighting a fire." ~W.B. Yeats

Mom's Coloring Time

Coloring beautiful pictures and doodling
relieves stress and helps with creativity & relaxation.

Reading Time

Sit down with a few books from your stack.

Write, draw or copy the things you want to remember.

Special Memories
Things that you want to remember...

A New Day!

My Verse, My Song or My Prayer...

_____
_____
_____
_____
_____
_____
_____
_____

What Matters Most...

_____
_____
_____
_____
_____

Prayer List

_____
_____
_____
_____
_____
_____
_____
_____

Mom's Coloring Time

Coloring beautiful pictures and doodling
relieves stress and helps with creativity & relaxation.

"The true sign of intelligence is not knowledge but imagination." ~ Albert Einstein

Plans & Perspective

"The home is the first and most effective place to learn the lessons of life: truth, honor, virtue, self control, the value of education, honest work, and the purpose and privilege of life." -McKay

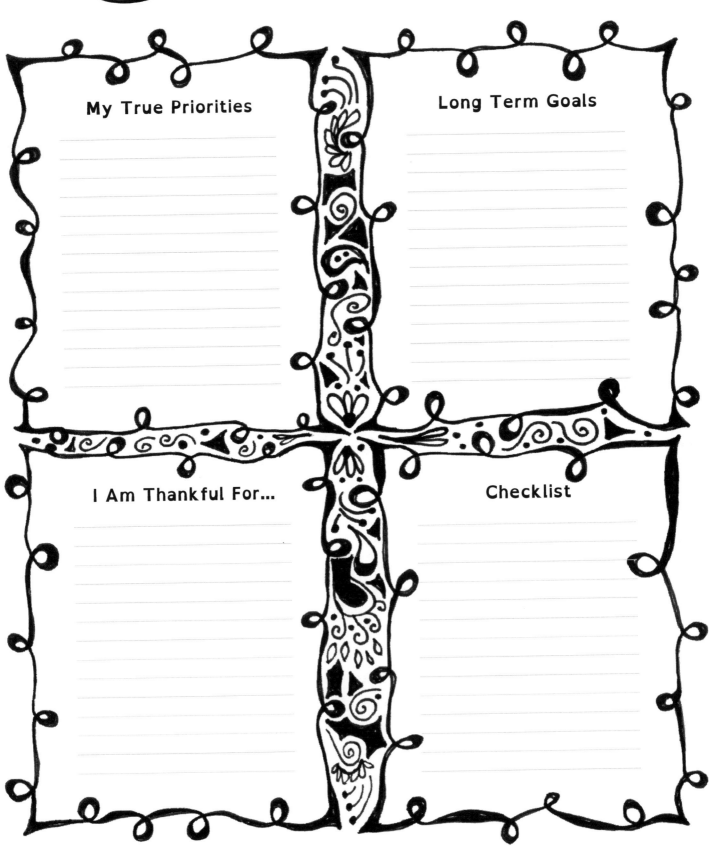

My True Priorities

Long Term Goals

I Am Thankful For...

Checklist

A New Day!

My Verse, My Song or My Prayer...

What Matters Most...

Prayer List

Mom's Coloring Time

Coloring beautiful pictures and doodling
relieves stress and helps with creativity & relaxation.

Plans & Perspective

"The home is the first and most effective place to learn the lessons of life: truth, honor, virtue, self control, the value of education, honest work, and the purpose and privilege of life." -McKay

My True Priorities

Long Term Goals

I Am Thankful For...

Checklist

A Vision for Your Life

What is your vision, and what are you doing to archive it in everyday life?

_____

_____

_____

_____

Your calling and purpose is unlike any other.
Ask God for His plans for your life. Ask God for wisdom,
guidance and strength to fulfill your purpose today.

Draw a picture of your dreams for this day,
for your future, for yourself, for your home,
your marriage or for your family.

Reading Time

Sit down with a few books from your stack.

Write, draw or copy the things you want to remember.

Mom's Illustrated TO-DO List

Mom's Coloring Time

Coloring beautiful pictures and doodling
relieves stress and helps with creativity & relaxation.

Ideas for Fun & Learning Together

Menu Planning

Open up an old-fashion cookbook!

_____

_____

_____

_____

_____

_____

Shopping List

_____

_____

_____

_____

_____

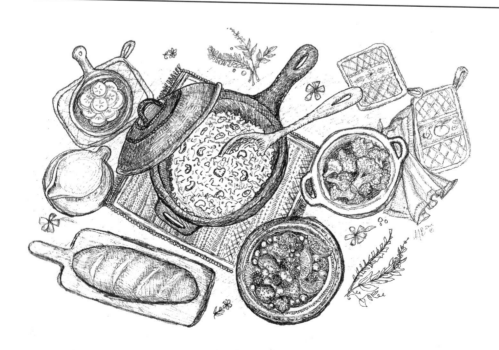

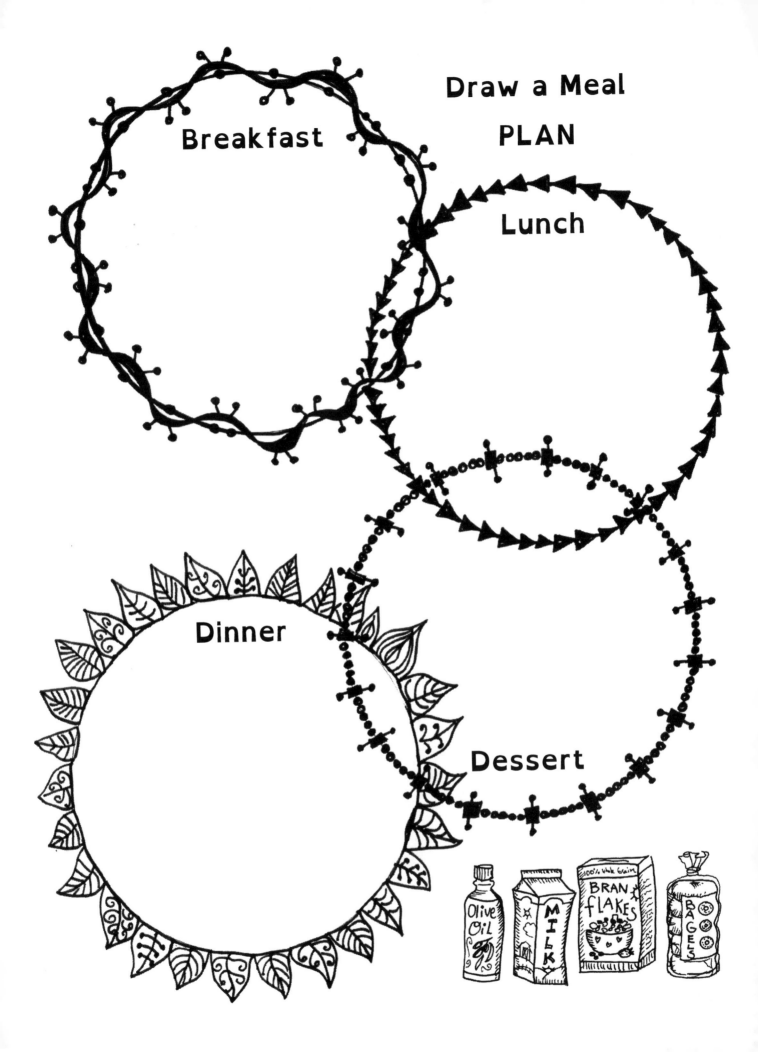

Breakfast

Draw a Meal
PLAN

Lunch

Dinner

Dessert

Mom's Coloring Time

Coloring beautiful pictures and doodling
relieves stress and helps with creativity & relaxation.

Recipe:

_____

Serves:

Prep Time:

Ingredients:

Instructions:

Shopping List:

"Recipe for genius: More of family and less of school, more of parents and less of peers, more creative freedom and less formal lessons." ~Raymond Moore

Mommy Math Time

Math is something that Kids need help with.

Go get a kid and show them how to do some math here:

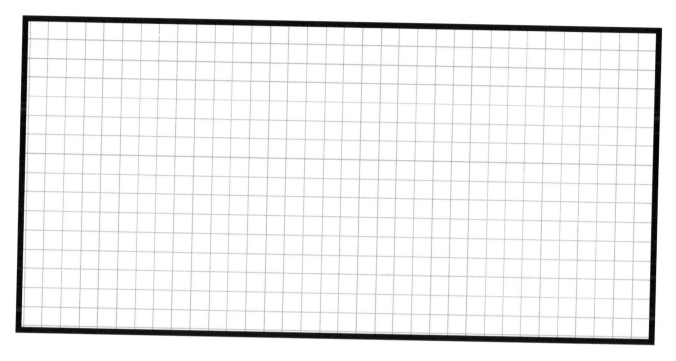

"Everything I am interested in, from cooking to electronics, is related to math. In real life you don't have to worry about integrating math into other subjects. In real life, math already is integrated into everything else." ~ Hoffstrom

Listening Time

Listen to an audio book or classical music or ask someone to read a story to you while you color and draw on the next page.

What are you listening to?

Reading Time

Sit down with a few books from your stack.

Write, draw or copy the things you want to remember.

TITLE:

STARS:

Screen Time! Watch a Documentary, Educational Program, Movie, or Tutorial.

My Review of this Film:

Draw a Scene from the video:

Rating:
AWFUL
BAD
LAME
YUCKY
OKAY
NICE
GOOD
GREAT
SUPER
AMAZING

World News Today!

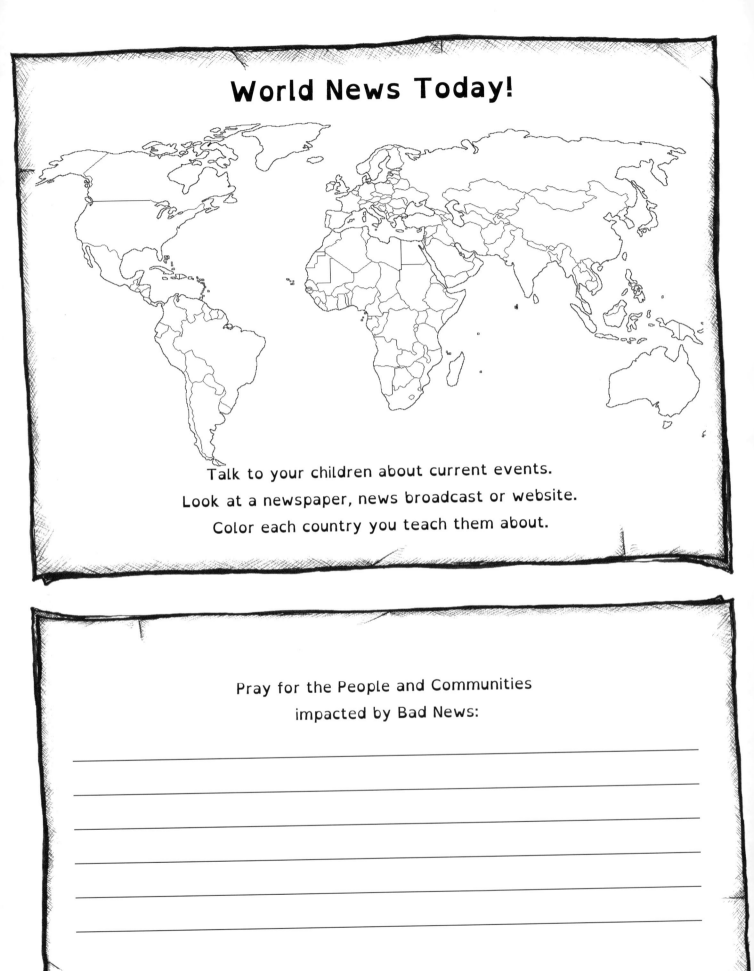

Talk to your children about current events.

Look at a newspaper, news broadcast or website.

Color each country you teach them about.

Pray for the People and Communities
impacted by Bad News:

_____

_____

_____

_____

_____

_____

Daily Journal

_____
_____
_____
_____
_____
_____
_____
_____
_____
_____
_____
_____

"Education is not filling a bucket,
but lighting a fire." ~W.B. Yeats

Special Memories

Things that you want to remember...

A New Day!

My Verse, My Song or My Prayer...

What Matters Most...

Prayer List

Mom's Coloring Time

Coloring beautiful pictures and doodling
relieves stress and helps with creativity & relaxation.

"The true sign of intelligence is not knowledge but imagination." ~ Albert Einstein

Plans & Perspective

"The home is the first and most effective place to learn the lessons of life: truth, honor, virtue, self control, the value of education, honest work, and the purpose and privilege of life." -McKay

My True Priorities

Long Term Goals

I Am Thankful For...

Checklist

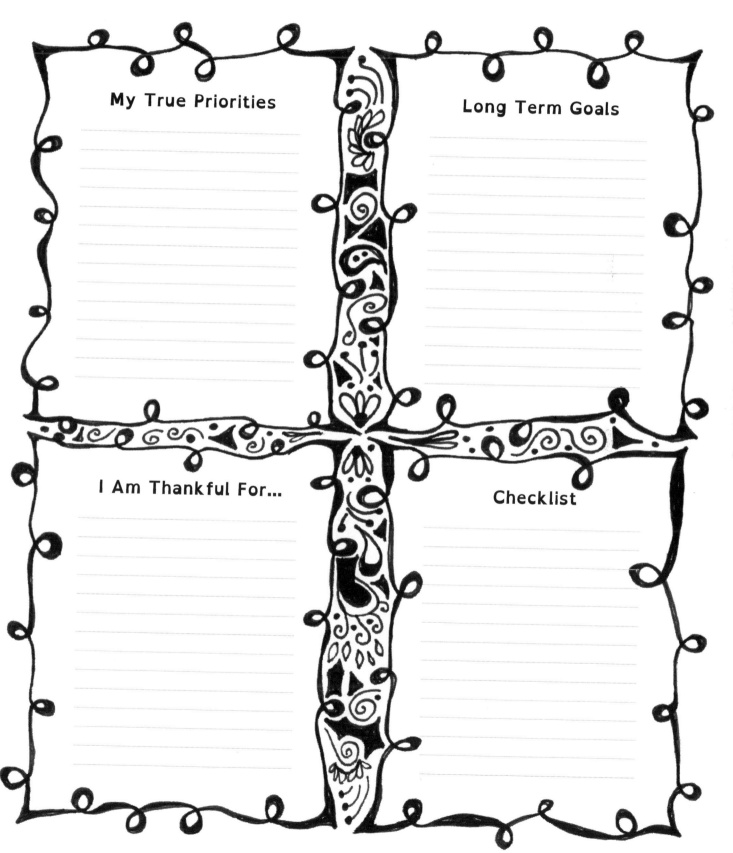

A New Day!

My Verse, My Song or My Prayer...

What Matters Most...

Prayer List

Mom's Coloring Time

Coloring beautiful pictures and doodling
relieves stress and helps with creativity & relaxation.

"The true sign of intelligence is not knowledge but imagination." ~ Albert Einstein

Plans & Perspective

"The home is the first and most effective place to learn the lessons of life: truth, honor, virtue, self control, the value of education, honest work, and the purpose and privilege of life." -McKay

My True Priorities

Long Term Goals

I Am Thankful For...

Checklist

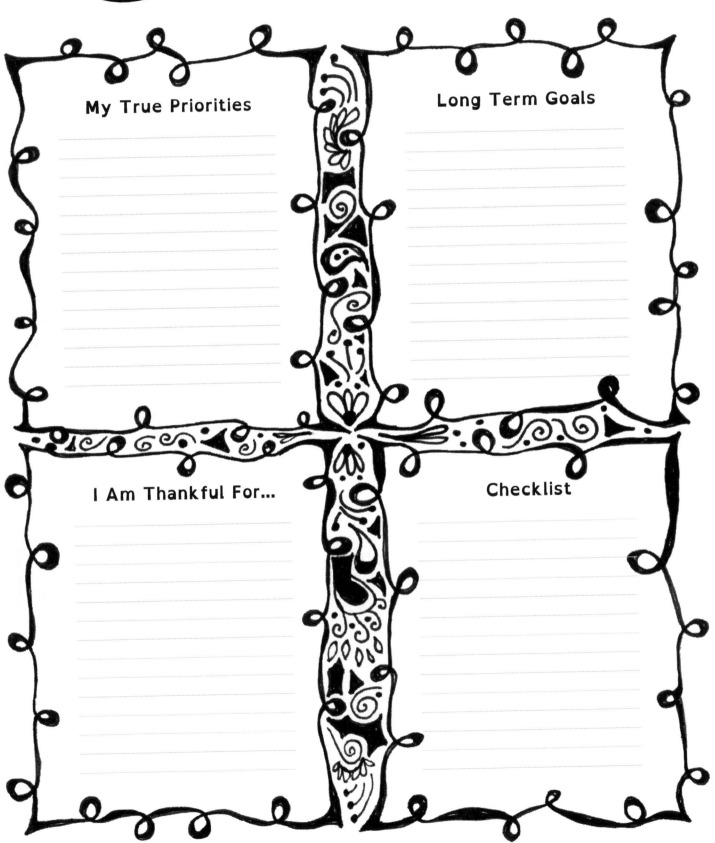

A Vision for Your Life

What is your vision, and what are you doing to archive it in everyday life?

_____

_____

_____

_____

Your calling and purpose is unlike any other.
Ask God for His plans for your life. Ask God for wisdom,
guidance and strength to fulfill your purpose today.

Draw a picture of your dreams for this day,
for your future, for yourself, for your home,
your marriage or for your family.

Reading Time

Sit down with a few books from your stack.

Write, draw or copy the things you want to remember.

Mom's Illustrated TO-DO List

Mom's Coloring Time

Coloring beautiful pictures and doodling
relieves stress and helps with creativity & relaxation.

Ideas for Fun & Learning Together

Menu Planning

Open up an old-fashion cookbook!

_____

_____

_____

_____

_____

_____

Shopping List

_____

_____

_____

_____

_____

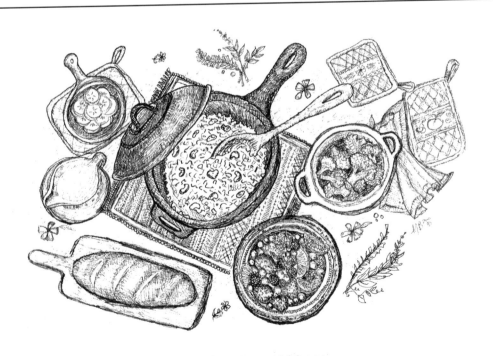

Breakfast

Draw a Meal
PLAN

Lunch

Dinner

Dessert

Recipe:

_____

Serves:

Prep Time:

Ingredients:

Instructions:

Shopping List:

"Recipe for genius: More of family and less of school, more of parents and less of peers, more creative freedom and less formal lessons." ~Raymond Moore

Mommy Math Time

Math is something that kids need help with.
Go get a kid and show them how to do some math here:

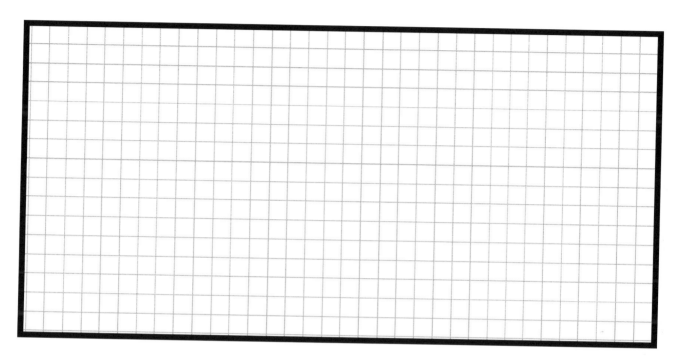

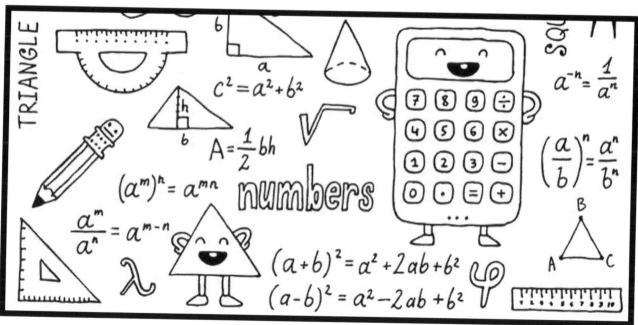

"Everything I am interested in, from cooking to electronics, is related to math. In real life you don't have to worry about integrating math into other subjects. In real life, math already is integrated into everything else." ~ Hoffstrom

Listening Time

Listen to an audio book or classical music or ask someone to read a story to you while you color and draw on the next page.

What are you listening to?

_____

Reading Time

Sit down with a few books from your stack.

Write, draw or copy the things you want to remember.

TITLE:

STARS:

Screen Time!

Watch a Documentary, Educational Program, Movie, or Tutorial.

My Review of this Film:

Draw a Scene from the video:

Rating:
AWFUL
BAD
LAME
YUCKY
OKAY
NICE
GOOD
GREAT
SUPER
AMAZING

World News Today!

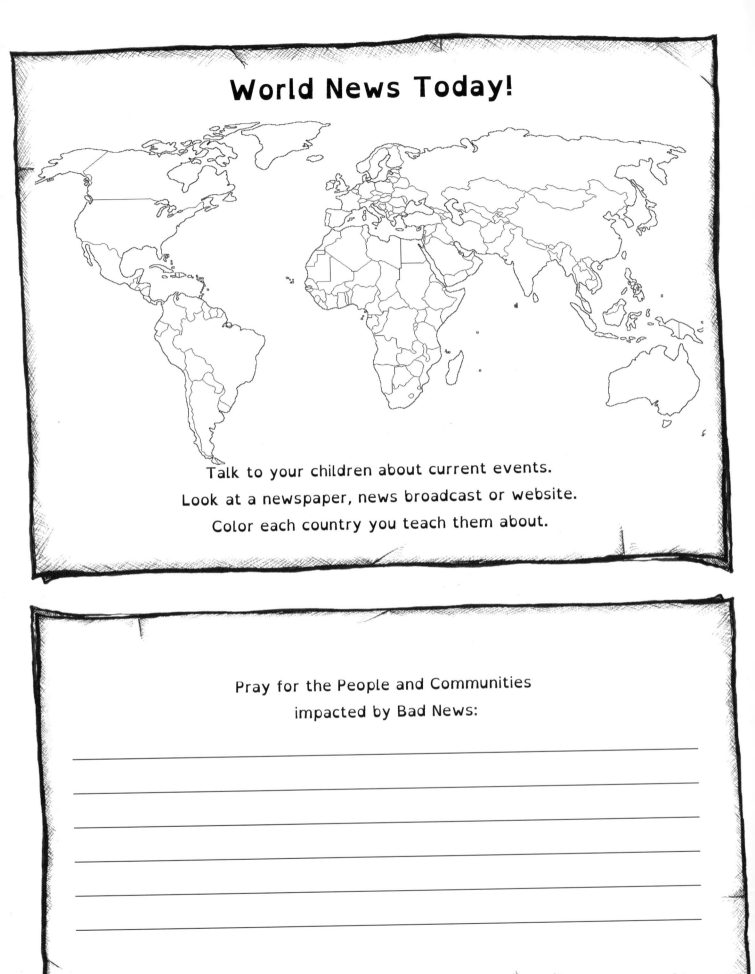

Talk to your children about current events.

Look at a newspaper, news broadcast or website.

Color each country you teach them about.

Pray for the People and Communities
impacted by Bad News:

_____

_____

_____

_____

_____

_____

Daily Journal

_____
_____
_____
_____
_____
_____
_____
_____
_____
_____
_____
_____

"Education is not filling a bucket,
but lighting a fire." ~W.B. Yeats

Special Memories

Things that you want to remember...

Reading Time

Sit down with a few books from your stack.

Write, draw or copy the things you want to remember.

Mom's Coloring Time

Coloring beautiful pictures and doodling
relieves stress and helps with creativity & relaxation.

Mom's Homeschooling Handbook

Copyright Information

Contact Us:

The Thinking Tree LLC

617 N. Swope St. Greenfield, IN 46140. United States

317.622.8852 PHONE (Dial +1 outside of the USA) 267.712.7889 FAX

Do-It-Yourself Homeschooling

www.DyslexiaGames.com

jbrown@DyslexiaGames.com

Made in the USA
San Bernardino, CA
24 April 2016